The Coconut Flour Gourmet

150 DELICIOUS GLUTEN-FREE COCONUT FLOUR RECIPES

Bruce Fife *and* Leslie Fife

Piccadilly Books, Ltd.
Colorado Springs, CO

Every effort has been made to ensure that the information contained in this book is complete and accurate. However, neither the publisher nor the author is engaged in rendering professional advice or services to the individual reader. The ideas, procedures, and suggestions contained in this book are not intended as a substitute for consulting with your physician. All matters regarding your health require medical supervision. Neither the publisher nor the author are responsible for your specific health or allergy needs that may require medical supervision and are not responsible for any adverse reactions to the recipes contained in this book.

Piccadilly Books, Ltd.
P.O. Box 25203
Colorado Springs, CO 80936, USA
info@piccadillybooks.com
www.piccadillybooks.com

Library of Congress Cataloging-in-Publication Data
Fife, Bruce, 1952-
    The coconut flour gourmet : 150 delicious gluten-free coconut flour recipes / by Bruce Fife and Leslie Fife.
        pages cm
    Includes index.
    ISBN-13: 978-0-941599-93-1 (pbk.)
    ISBN-10: 0-941599-93-0 (pbk.)
    1. Cooking (Coconut flour) 2. Gluten-free diet--Recipes. 3. Cookbooks.
lcgft I. Fife, Leslie, 1957- II Title.
    TX814.5.C63F52 2013
    641.6'461--dc23
                                                        2012043551
Published in the USA

Contents

Coconut Flour Basics

THE STORY OF COCONUT FLOUR
Where Does Coconut Flour Come From?

In 2004 my wife Leslie and I were invited to the Philippines to lecture on the health benefits and uses of virgin coconut oil. As the directors of the Coconut Research Center, we often travel around the world lecturing on various health aspects of coconut. While we were in the Philippines we had the opportunity to visit several coconut processing facilities and see the entire process from the harvesting of the coconuts on the farms to the labeling of the finished product. Although several methods are used to produce virgin coconut oil, the most popular procedure starts with grating the meat from fresh coconuts. The grated meat is then put in a large dehydrator to evaporate the water. The dried coconut is next placed into a press—often a small, hand operated press. The coconut oil is squeezed out of the dried coconut, then filtered and heat- or vacuum-processed in order to purify the product and reduce the moisture content.

After the oil is pressed out of the meat, what remains is the defatted, dehydrated coconut meal. It has a texture similar to that of corn meal and still contains a high concentration of vitamins, minerals, proteins, carbohydrates, and other nutrients. Sometimes it is used like dried desiccated coconut for making candy and desserts. However, since all of the water and nearly all of the oil has been removed, the meal is fairly tasteless and isn't often used. Dried desiccated or shredded coconut is more flavorful, is easier to find in stores, and is generally preferred in cooking.

Generally, the leftover coconut meal is sold as a high quality animal feed or used as an organic fertilizer to enrich farm soils. Income from these types of sales is minimal, though. Since selling the meal for human consumption offers a potentially higher profit, eventually researchers tried grinding coconut meal into a fine powder to produce a product with the consistency of flour. Thus, coconut flour was created.

The flour was originally developed by researchers at the Philippine Coconut Authority, a division of the Philippine Department of Agriculture, who experimented with it in baking and food preparation. Coconut flour looks, feels, smells, and even tastes very similar to wheat and other grain flours. However, the physical characteristics are dramatically different. Coconut flour does not perform the same as wheat flour in bread making and baking. The properties of coconut flour are so different from wheat flour that it is impossible to use as a wheat flour substitute. The only way the researchers were able to use it with standard recipes was to replace no more than 20 percent of the wheat flour with coconut flour. If much more than 20 percent is used in any recipe, the resulting product will be a complete disaster. Coconut flour was a good idea, but it turned out to be impractical as a wheat substitute using *standard* wheat recipes. There was a need to develop recipes designed specifically for the unique characteristics of coconut flour. Until recently, nobody had tried doing this.

Why Is Coconut Flour Good for Me?
Coconut flour has several desirable characteristics which make it a promising bakery product. It is a good source of a variety of nutrients, including protein. It contains about 10 to 12 percent protein, which is the same as whole wheat flour. It is also an excellent source of dietary fiber. In fact, coconut flour consists of about 60 percent fiber: this is nearly five times as much as whole wheat flour and more than twice as much as wheat bran. Another benefit of coconut flour is its mild taste. You would think that it might taste like coconut, but it doesn't. In fact, it is nearly tasteless. When coconut flour is used in baking, you cannot detect any coconut flavor. It takes on the flavor of the other ingredients used in the recipe such as lemon, strawberry, or chocolate. Of course, if you want the coconut taste you can add shredded coconut or coconut flavoring just as you would with wheat flour.

The primary benefit of coconut flour is its complete absence of gluten. Gluten is the primary protein found in wheat and some other grains such as rye and barley. The problem with gluten is that many people are highly sensitive to it and need to avoid it for health reasons.

Despite all of these wonderful characteristics, coconut flour does require a bit of care when using in recipes, as it does not perform like wheat flour and cannot be simply substituted in a 1:1 ratio like some other flours. But this is not a concern for you, as all of the recipes in this book have been specifically developed with the special qualities of coconut flour in mind—so all you need to do is follow the simple directions provided.

Amazingly Good Coconut Flour Recipes
When I learned about the existence of coconut flour I could see its potential. There are millions of people who are allergic to wheat or

sensitive to gluten who would love to have an alternative to wheat flour. However, at that time, there were no recipes available. No one really knew how to use coconut flour effectively. It could replace a small portion of wheat flour in recipes, but that doesn't help people who are allergic to wheat.

By a process of trial and error I slowly developed a number of basic formulas that gave good results. I learned what worked and what didn't. With a little refining and in some cases the addition of some other types of gluten-free flours, I was able to make a variety of breads, cakes, muffins, cookies, and other baked goods that tasted every bit as good as those made with wheat flour.

For the most part, the recipes in this book are very simple. I like simple, because cooking is fun when it only takes a few minutes to bake a cake or turn out a dozen cookies. These recipes are unique. Each recipe in this book had to be created from scratch using a completely different approach than that used in wheat-based recipes, so you won't find them anywhere else.

The popularity of coconut flour over the past few years has been remarkable. When I started this project several years ago there were absolutely no coconut flour recipes available, even though coconut flour had been around for a number of years. No one ever used it because they simply didn't know how. With the creation of my recipes and the publication of my book *Cooking with Coconut Flour: A Delicious Low-Carb, Gluten-Free Alternative to Wheat,* a market for coconut flour was born. Coconut flour is now available in virtually every health food store as well as on the Internet. Even some large supermarket chains keep it in stock.

Since the publication of that book many people have asked for more gluten-free coconut flour recipes and specifically yeast-based recipes. In response, my wife and I teamed up to create more than 150 totally new recipes. In the previous book, only coconut flour was used. This prevented the inclusion of yeast-based recipes. For this new book, we placed no restriction on carbohydrate content, thus allowing us to add higher carb flours and develop a variety of gluten-free yeast breads and other baked goods.

The recipes in this book are designed to appeal to a wide variety of tastes. If you like occasional sweets and after dinner desserts, there are plenty here to choose from. You will find cakes, cupcakes, tarts, cookies, and even ice cream sandwiches. We've made the recipes adaptable enough that you can cater the recipes to your preferences. If you would like to use less sugar or a different type of sweetener than that specified in the recipes, feel free to do so. You will also find plenty of breads and savory items such as meats, main dishes, pancakes, waffles, and muffins (yes, pancakes, waffles, and muffins can be savory!). Every recipe in this book is made using coconut flour and is completely gluten-free.

GETTING TO KNOW YOUR INGREDIENTS

Before jumping into the recipe section, let's quickly highlight a few of the main ingredients used in the recipes, so you know how each functions and why it's needed. This will make it easier to not only make every recipe successfully but also to adapt and substitute ingredients as you please.

Coconut Flour

If you are an experienced cook, you are probably familiar with the appearance and texture of a variety of baked goods. You can tell when the dough has enough liquid just by its appearance and feel. With coconut flour, however, the texture and feel of the batter will be a little different. You cannot judge how a coconut flour recipe is going to turn out based on your experience with wheat flour. For this reason, I highly recommend that you follow the directions in these recipes exactly as they are given. Once you become familiar with using coconut flour, then feel free to do some experimenting and make adjustments.

That said, sometimes altitude, humidity, oven temperature, or quality of the coconut flour or other ingredients you are using can influence the outcome. If you follow the directions precisely as given, but still feel the product was a little too dry or moist, try adjusting the recipe slightly. Add a little more flour or liquid, or try adjusting the cooking time.

Since coconut flour is high in fiber, it is very absorbent. The flour will even pull moisture out of the air. Once the package is opened, it is best to store unused flour in an airtight container. You can store coconut flour at room temperature (about 70°F/21°C) for at least a year. If you live in a warm climate you may want to store it in the refrigerator to extend its shelf life.

Because coconut flour tends to absorb moisture from the atmosphere, it often develops small lumps. These lumps will make your batter lumpy if you don't remove them first. To remove the lumps it is a good idea to routinely sift the flour before adding it in any recipe. All the measurements listed in this book are made *before* sifting. Measure out the amount called for in the recipe, sift it, and then add it to the other ingredients as directed.

Flour Combinations

When we were developing the recipes for this book, one of our initial goals was to use coconut flour as the primary flour. However, in some cases, we have added other gluten-free flours to take advantage of their special characteristics. While all of the recipes contain coconut flour, a few will also contain some other gluten-free flours such as almond flour or rice flour.

For baked goods that normally use baking powder as a leavening agent (e.g., cakes, pancakes, muffins, and cookies), coconut flour alone works very well. However, yeast breads are another matter. We have been unsuccessful in producing good quality yeast breads using only coconut flour. However, by taking advantage of the characteristics of a few other flours and combining them with coconut flour, we have been able to produce a variety of delightful yeast breads. With the basic yeast dough recipe described in this book you will be able to make gluten-free yeast breads that remind you of your mother's homemade baked bread. These recipes include sandwich bread, dinner rolls, hamburger buns, bread sticks, scones, and even pizza crust, among others.

Gluten Replacers

One of the difficulties of using coconut flour in baking is the lack of gluten. It is the gluten in wheat that makes it possible to have the breads with their familiar taste and texture. Gluten gives dough its elastic texture and traps air bubbles when rising and baking, making the bread light and airy. Without gluten, breads would be hard and dense and much less appetizing and tasteful.

Certain water soluble plant fibers such as xanthan gum and guar gum take on a sticky gelatinous character when combined with water and perform much like gluten in baked goods. We use xanthan gum in the yeast breads described in this book. Rice flour is also used because when combined with heat and water, it develops a sticky texture that helps trap air bubbles.

Eggs can also be used as a substitute for gluten. Eggs function as a binder to trap air bubbles and act as a leavening agent as well. Eggs are a powerhouse of nutrition and enrich baked goods with many important nutrients. They supply a high-quality protein with a full range of amino acids. Eggs also contain a wide spectrum of important nutrients such as vitamins A, D, B_6, B_{12}, thiamin, riboflavin, and niacin; minerals calcium, magnesium, potassium, zinc, and selenium; and essential fatty acids, including the omega-3 fatty acid DHA. Egg yolk is a natural source of lecithin, which is useful for emulsifying and blending together the fat-soluble and water-soluble ingredients in the recipes. Additionally, lecithin is a source of choline, a vitamin essential for proper brain function.

Egg yolk also contains cholesterol, which is used by the body to form many of our hormones and is necessary for the production of vitamin D. There is no need to worry about the cholesterol in eggs being harmful. Studies have repeatedly shown that eggs have no detrimental effect on blood cholesterol levels, even when consumed in large quantities. In fact, recent studies show that eating eggs increases your HDL (good) cholesterol improving your cholesterol ratio, thus *reducing* your risk of heart disease. Eggs are actually a superfood! For these reasons, eggs are used in many of the recipes in this book and greatly enhance the protein and nutritional content of the recipes.

Sweeteners

Being a nutritionist, I am very aware of the problems of eating too much sugar, especially highly processed and refined sugars. However, many breads and baked goods require some type of sweetening. The purpose of this book is to provide an alternative to wheat and show you how to use coconut flour to make a variety of delicious baked goods. Consequently, the recipes in this book include many desserts and sweets in addition to the savory dishes to appeal to a wide audience with varying needs and preferences.

I prefer to use natural sweeteners such as honey, coconut sugar, date sugar, maple sugar, dehydrated sugarcane juice (Sucanat, muscovado, rapadura), molasses, and the like. I do not recommend the use of artificial sweeteners such as NutriSweet (aspartame) or Splenda (sucralose). None of the recipes in this book are formulated to use artificial sweeteners.

There is a wide selection of natural, seminatural, and conventional sweeteners to choose from. Due to diet limitations and personal preferences, some people prefer certain types of sweeteners over others. Most of the recipes in this book are versatile enough so that you can use the sweetener of your choice. Generally, when the term "sugar" is used in any of the recipes in this book you can substitute any type of *dry* sweetener such as granulated white sugar, coconut sugar, Sucanat, xylitol, or other dry sweetener. When the term "honey" is used in a recipe, you can use honey or substitute any *liquid* sweetener, such as corn syrup, maple syrup, and so forth. Making substitutions can alter the taste and sweetness somewhat, but you can adjust this to your taste. However, if a particular type of sweetener is recommended in a recipe, it will be mentioned by name. If the recipe calls for brown sugar, for instance, it is recommend that you use this type of sweetener or something very similar to it.

There are a couple of exceptions to this substitution rule: molasses and stevia. Molasses can have a very pronounced effect on the flavor of a recipe. For this reason, you should only use it if the recipe specifically calls for it. Stevia is a zero calorie herbal sweetener and is much sweeter than sugar. A spoonful has the sweetening effect of a cup of sugar, so a little can go a long way. You have to be careful with stevia because if you use too much it will give your food a strong bitter aftertaste. To avoid the aftertaste, only a modest amount of stevia can be used. For this reason, stevia usually needs to be combined with another sweetener to give baked goods the sweetness needed. Sugar not only sweetens baked goods but is also important for providing bulk and texture, so the volume used is an important factor in the success of any recipe. Replacing sugar with a smaller volume of stevia can significantly alter the texture and outcome of the recipes, so it is not recommended as a replacement for the sugar in these recipes.

Fats and Oils

Fats and oils add tenderness and flavor to baked goods. While we often talk about fats and oils as if they were two separate things, technically there is no difference. All fats are oils and vice versa. However, generally speaking, we call something a fat if it is solid at room temperature and an oil if it is liquid.

12

In these recipes coconut oil or butter are most commonly specified. However, you can use any type of oil you prefer. The oils I recommend for cooking are coconut oil, palm oil, butter, and even animal fat. You can use coconut oil for nearly all the recipes in this book. In some recipes, though, a particular type of oil may be recommended. In such cases the recipe will turn out better if you use the oil specified.

I like to use coconut oil because of its many health properties and because it remains stable under normal cooking temperatures. If you are not familiar with using coconut oil I need to point out one distinguishing characteristic: it has a relatively high melting point. At temperatures above 76°F (25°C), the oil is a clear liquid much like any other vegetable oil. But below this temperature it starts to harden into a white solid. Butter does the same thing. If you put it in the refrigerator it becomes hard, but if you take it out on a hot day and set it on the kitchen counter it will eventually melt into a puddle. If you store the coconut oil in the cupboard it may be either liquid or solid depending on the temperature in your house. When using coconut oil in the recipes it should be melted but not hot. You can melt it quickly on the stove by putting some in a glass jar or saucepan.

One of the primary functions of cooking oil is to act as a lubricant to prevent sticking. In baking, sticking can be a real problem. Oiling or greasing of the baking dish, muffin tin, or cookie sheet is important. The type of oil you use is also important. You can use non-stick pans, but I don't use them. I don't have a problem with breads sticking to pans because I use a special non-stick cooking oil that my wife and I developed. It's made from a combination of coconut oil and lecithin. This oil performs remarkably well. Nothing sticks to the pan and cleanup is often as simple as wiping the pan with a washcloth. Even hard, blackened, burned on crust wipes off with ease. No other oil comes close. It works better and cleans up faster than non-stick pans.

For lack of a better name I call it "Dr. Fife's Non-Stick Cooking Oil." You can make your own non-stick cooking oil by mixing together ½ cup (64 g) of melted coconut oil with 1 teaspoon of liquid lecithin (available at your health food store or online). Mix up a batch and use it as needed. I recommend that you use this oil for all of your baking. Use

---

Dr. Fife's Non-Stick Cooking Oil
Mix ½ cup (64 g) coconut oil with 1 teaspoon liquid lecithin.

---

what you need and store the remainder in the refrigerator. It will harden in the refrigerator but will last well over a year. To soften, just take it out of the refrigerator 30 minutes to an hour before you need to use it. If you use it frequently, though, you won't even need to refrigerate it. You will use it up long before it could spoil.

We use coconut oil in our house for almost all of our cooking and baking needs. It is an excellent cooking oil and has many health benefits associated with it. For more information about the health effects of coconut oil I recommend that you visit our educational website at www. coconutresearchcenter.org.

Nutrition Facts
Each recipe includes nutrition facts listing the total number of calories and grams of fat, carbohydrate, and, protein per serving. The total carbohydrate amount is further divided into fiber and net carbohydrate content. Fiber, which is a form of carbohydrate, supplies no calories. Removing the grams of fiber from the total carbohydrate amount leaves you with net carbohydrate—the amount of carbohydrate that does supply calories.

Nutrition information is based on serving size. The size will vary depending on the recipe and the yield. A single serving would constitute one slice, waffle, pancake, or muffin. For smaller portions the serving size will be given in measurements based on cups or grams.

All of the recipes in this book use healthy natural sources of fat. Fat gives food flavor and improves texture so we use it generously in many of the recipes. The nutrition facts will reflect this. This is not a low-fat cookbook. If you want to use less fat, in many cases you can reduce the amount specified to suit your preferences.

Yeast Breads

When people stop eating wheat the thing they usually miss the most is yeast bread—the bread you use to make sandwiches and toast and eat with butter or jam. Breads can be made without yeast, but they need some other type of leavening, like baking powder. Although baking powder products can taste very good, they can't truly take the place of yeast breads. There is just something about yeast breads that can't be matched by baking powder breads.

Creating good tasting gluten-free yeast breads is a challenge. Most of the gluten-free yeast breads we've tried have paled in comparison to wheat-based breads. However, after much experimentation, we succeeded in creating a formula that combines coconut flour with a few other gluten-free flours to produce one of the best tasting homemade gluten-free yeast breads we have ever tried.

When we were developing our basic yeast bread recipe we experimented with different types of flours, cooking times, temperatures, and numerous other variables. After much experimenting we narrowed down the recipe to what we felt worked the best. When the first loaf of our final version came out of the oven we could hardly wait to try it. One of our friends just happened to be visiting at the time so we offered him a slice of our experimental bread. He gladly accepted. We handed him a slice and asked, "Tell us what you think of it?" He took a big bite and began chewing. The first word out of his mouth was an enthusiastic, "Mmmmm!" The second word out of his mouth was also "Mmmm." And the third word was "Mmmm." Enough said, we knew the recipe was a success. When we tasted the bread ourselves, our reactions were the same. This was without question the best homemade gluten-free bread we had ever eaten. Right out of the oven it was just as good as freshly made wheat bread. Yum!

Our yeast bread formula uses a mix of coconut flour and three other gluten-free flours. This mix can be used as an all-purpose flour mix to make a variety of yeast-based breads, including sandwich bread, rolls, bread sticks, pizza crust, and more.

Coconut Gluten-Free (CGF) Flour Mix

Our basic flour mix is made from whole brown rice, coconut, millet, and tapioca flours. Tapioca flour, also known as tapioca starch, is a product derived from the root of the cassava plant. Millet is a small pale yellow seed grown in many parts of the world, particularly India and Africa.

These flours are combined into what we call our coconut gluten-free flour mix or *CGF Flour Mix*. This is the basic flour mix that is used in all of the yeast bread recipes in this chapter and even some of the baking powder recipes in other chapters. This mix contains far more vitamins, minerals, protein, and fiber than refined wheat flour. The formula is as follows:

3½ parts brown rice flour
2 parts coconut flour
2 parts millet flour
1½ parts tapioca flour

Combine all flours together. The mix uses "parts" instead of exact measurements so that you can make as much or as little of the mix as you want. We suggest you make enough to make several recipes: for example, use 1 cup as your "part" and you will have a total of 9 cups of baking mix. Keep the mix stored in an airtight container and use it whenever it's called for in the recipes in this book. It can be stored ready to use in your cupboard for several months.

All of these flours are sold in health food stores, online, and in some major grocery stores. Millet flour is available in most health food stores but is not as common as the other flours. In some areas, whole millet is easier to find. You can easily make your own millet flour from whole millet using a coffee grinder. Grind the millet seeds using the fine setting on your coffee grinder or to about the same grain size as brown rice flour.

Preparing the Dough
The following procedure is used for preparing the dough for all the yeast bread recipes in this book using the CGF Flour Mix. The amount of CGF flour and other ingredients will vary, but the procedure is the same for each recipe. Any differences will be noted in each individual recipe.

I recommend the use of fast-acting yeast in place of regular active dry yeast because it gives excellent results in a shorter amount of time. Fast-acting yeast is also known as rapid-rise, quick rise, instant, or bread machine yeast. You can use active dry yeast but if you do, you may need to allow extra time for the dough to rise appropriately. Wheat-based yeast breads usually require kneading the dough and two or more periods of rising and more kneading. The whole process takes several hours for a single batch of bread. Bread making using our CGF flour mix and fast-acting yeast requires no kneading and a single relatively brief period of rising, so you can make baked goods in half the time and with less effort.

Begin the dough making process by activating the yeast. Using the measurements specified in each recipe, mix the yeast and sugar into very warm water (about 110°F/45°C) and let it sit for about 5 to 8 minutes. As it sits, it should gradually start to bubble and foam. This indicates the yeast is activating and is feeding on the sugar. If the yeast does not foam or become frothy after a few minutes, the yeast is not activating. This can happen if your water was too hot, in which case it killed the yeast, or if the yeast was old or mostly dead before you used it. Always check the expiration date on the package. While the yeast is activating, prepare the rest of the recipe.

In a large mixing bowl, blend together CGF Flour Mix, xanthan gum, salt, baking powder, and any other dry ingredient listed in the recipe. In a small bowl, whisk together eggs and coconut oil or other oil as specified in each recipe. If the recipe calls for coconut oil, the eggs need to be at room temperature so they don't cause the oil to harden. Add the wet ingredients, including the activated yeast, to the dry ingredients and mix together using an electric mixer for about 2 to 3 minutes. Periodically scrape down the dough from the sides of the mixing bowl to thoroughly blend. The dough will be soft.

Each recipe will specify how to shape the dough and in what types of pans it should be put into for rising. Once prepared, put the dough-filled pan in a warm place and allow it to rise. It can be placed in a warm (about 110°-120°F/45°-50°C) oven. If you put the dough in the oven to rise, be careful as too high of a temperature will kill the yeast. Allow the dough to rise until it doubles in size. This should take roughly 30 to 45 minutes depending on the temperature where the bread is rising.

If you put the dough in the oven for rising, remove it before preheating the oven for baking. Cook the dough as directed in each recipe.

Tips on Greasing Pans
When baking breads it is important that you grease the pan to prevent sticking. We highly recommend that you use Dr. Fife's Non-Stick

Cooking Oil described on page 13. With this oil all you have to do once the bread is finished cooking is to turn it upside down on a wire rack. The bread will then fall out of the pan almost effortlessly. The pan will be clean with no burnt spots or sticking and will wash in just a few seconds. If you don't use this non-stick oil, you can use any other oil you prefer. After greasing the pan with other oils, you need to lightly dust it with rice flour or CGF Flour Mix before adding the dough. Additionally, after baking a knife may be needed to coax the bread out of the pan.

Leslie's Sandwich Bread

This gluten-free sandwich bread tastes just as good as any homemade wheat-based sandwich bread. It tastes incredibly delicious right out of the oven with just a dab of butter or honey butter. This recipe uses fast-acting yeast, so rising only takes 30 to 45 minutes. Using this recipe you can make as many as four loaves of bread (depending on the size of your oven) in as little as an hour and a half.

1 tablespoon (8.5 g) fast-acting yeast
3 tablespoons (39 g) sugar

1 cup plus 2 tablespoons (270 ml) very warm water
2½ cups (340 g) CGF Flour Mix (page 16)
1 tablespoon (9 g) xanthan gum
1½ teaspoons salt
1 teaspoon baking powder
3 eggs at room temperature
2 tablespoons (28 g) coconut oil, melted

Make the dough using the above measurements according to the Preparing the Dough section on page 17.

Put a little coconut oil on your fingers to prevent sticking, then roll the dough on a flat surface that has been dusted with CGF flour and mold into a loaf shape. Place the dough into an 8.5 x 4.5 x 2.5 inch (22 x 11 x 6 cm) greased loaf pan, preferably one made of glass. It should fill the pan about three-quarters full. Using a sharp knife, cut three or four slits about ¼ inch (6 mm) deep across the top of the dough. This will allow the dough to expand evenly and will add a decorative touch.

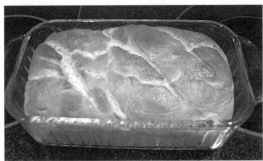

Put the dough-filled pan in a warm place and to rise. Allow the dough to rise about ½ inch (1.25 cm) above the top of the pan. This should take about 45 minutes depending on the temperature.

Preheat the oven to 350°F (180°C or gas mark 4). Bake for 35 to 40 minutes or until the top is a dark golden brown and the bread springs back quickly when pressed. Take the loaf out of the oven and let it cool for at least 15 minutes before removing it from the baking pan. This will allow time for the loaf to set and retain its shape. If the loaf is removed too early it has a tendency to shrink a bit in volume as it cools.

This recipe makes one loaf of bread. If you want to make two, three, or four loaves at a time, you can double, triple, or quadruple the recipe. However, we don't recommend that you make too many loaves at one time unless you plan on using them within three or four days. The sandwich bread tastes best when it is freshly made. See storage tip below.

Yield: 1 loaf (about 14 slices)
Per slice: 4g fat, 22.4g total carbohydrate (3.1g fiber, 19.3g net carb), 3.4g protein, 137 calories.

Storage Tip: Coconut gluten-free sandwich bread tends to retain moisture, which can cause it to become doughy when stored overnight in an airtight container or plastic bag. You can prevent this by allowing the bread to "season" for a few hours before storing it. After the

bread has cooled, cut the entire loaf into sandwich size slices. Spread each slice out on a cooling rack to allow excess moisture to evaporate. Keep the slices on the rack until they start to feel dry. This may take several hours depending on the humidity. If you live in a humid area you may want to season the bread in a warm oven. After the slices have dried slightly, gather them together into a loaf and store it in a plastic bag or other container. Although the bread may feel a little dry at this point, it will regain a soft texture while stored. If you follow this procedure, your bread will store much better and taste fresh longer.

If the bread becomes too dry or "stale" don't throw it away. Leftover bread can be eaten in many ways. "Day-old" bread can be used in the following recipes in this book:

Croutons (page 25)
Leslie's Bread Crumbs (page 26)
Gluten-Free French Toast (page 72)
Bread and Butter Pudding (page 119)
Apricot Almond Bread Pudding (page 120)
Cinnamon Crisps (page 142)
Sesame Pecan Chicken with Hiosin Sauce (page 149)
Stuffed Bell Peppers (page 152)
Zucchini Boats (page 155)
Mighty-Good Meatloaf (page 158)
Turkey Stuffing (page 161)
Chicken and Zucchini Casserole (page 168)

Artisan Sandwich Bread

This is similar to Leslie's Sandwich Bread but is baked on a baking sheet without a pan. Brushing on a coating of egg gives the bread a glossy look when it is finished cooking and allows the sesame seeds to adhere to the dough. Although not required, the sesame seeds add a great touch and taste fantastic.

1 tablespoon (8.5 g) fast-acting yeast
3 tablespoons (39 g) sugar
1 cup plus 2 tablespoons (270 ml) very warm water
2½ cups (340 g) CGF Flour Mix (page 16)
1 tablespoon (9 g) xanthan gum
1½ teaspoons salt
1 teaspoon baking powder
3 eggs at room temperature

2 tablespoons (28 g) butter, melted
1 egg, beaten (optional)
Sesame seeds (optional)

Make the dough using the first nine ingredients according to the Preparing the Dough section on page 17.

Put a little coconut oil on your fingers to prevent sticking and roll the dough in a ball. Place the ball of dough onto the center of a greased baking sheet. Using a sharp knife cut three or four slits about ¼ inch (6 mm) deep across the top of the dough. This will allow the dough to expand without causing rips or tears and add a decorative touch.

Place the dough and baking sheet in a warm place to rise. Allow the dough to double in size. This should take about 45 minutes depending on the temperature. We like to put the bread in a warm oven and check it periodically.

Preheat the oven to 350°F (180°C or gas mark 4). If you put the bread in the oven to rise, make sure to remove it before preheating the oven. Using a pastry brush, *gently* coat the top and sides of the dough

with the beaten egg. If desired, you can sprinkle sesame seeds over the dough.

Bake for 35 to 40 minutes or until the top of the loaf is a dark golden brown and the bread springs back quickly when pressed. Remove the bread from the oven and let cool on a wire rack. Store leftover bread using the tip on page 21.

Yield: 1 loaf (about 14 slices)
Per serving: 4g fat, 22.4g total carbohydrate (3.1g fiber, 19.3g net carb), 3.4g protein, 137 calories.

Garlic Toast

This recipe is for those people who miss eating garlic bread. This gluten free recipe uses Leslie's Sandwich Bread and is toasted in a skillet. Adjust the amount of garlic and onion powder to suit your taste.

2 tablespoons (28 g) butter, softened
¼ teaspoon garlic powder
⅛ teaspoon onion powder
2 slices Leslie's Sandwich Bread (page 19)

Mix together butter, garlic powder, and onion powder. Spread butter mixture on one side of two slices of bread. Put each slice of bread into a hot skillet, butter side down. While the first side is cooking, butter the top side. When the bottom side is toasted, flip and toast the other side. Remove from skillet and enjoy.

Yield: 2 slices of garlic toast
Per slice: 15.5g fat, 22.4g total carbohydrate (3.1g fiber, 19.3g net carb), 3.4g protein, 239 calories.

Double Grilled Cheese Sandwich

Remember the grilled cheese sandwiches you had as a child? Here is a gluten-free version using Leslie's Sandwich Bread. This sandwich is "double grilled," meaning each slice of bread is pan toasted on both sides. For a cheesier sandwich add another ounce (14 g) slice of cheese.

24

3 tablespoons (42 g) butter
2 slices Leslie's Sandwich Bread (page 19)
2 ounces (28 g) sliced cheese

Spread butter on one side of two slices of bread. Put each slice of bread into a hot skillet, butter side down. While the first side is cooking, butter the top side of each slice. When the bottom side is toasted, flip one slice of bread and layer cheese on the toasted side. Place the other slice of bread on top, with the toasted side on the cheese. Finish by toasting the remaining side of the sandwich.

Yield: 1 sandwich
Per serving: 61.3g fat, 45.6g total carbohydrate (6.2g fiber, 39.4g net carb), 21.3g protein, 808 calories.

Croutons

Croutons add flavor and crunch to salads, soups, and casseroles. They can be made ahead of time and stored in an airtight container or frozen and reheated. This is a good way to use day-old gluten-free bread.

2 tablespoons (28 g) butter, softened
½ teaspoon onion powder
6 slices of day old Leslie's Sandwich Bread (page 19)

Preheat oven to 300°F (150°C or gas mark 2). Blend butter and onion powder together. Trim the crust off the bread and discard. Coat one side of each slice of bread with butter mixture. Cut the bread into ½ inch (1.25 cm) cubes. Spread cubes evenly on an ungreased baking sheet. Bake for 20 minutes, turn, and bake for another 15 minutes or until the bread is light golden brown and crispy. Remove from oven and let cool for at least 1 hour.

Yield: 2 cups (160 g) of croutons
Per ¼ cup serving: 5.9g fat, 16.8g total carbohydrate (2.3g fiber, 14.5g net carb), 2.6g protein, 128 calories.

Variation: Give the croutons an Italian flavor by adding to the butter mixture ¼ teaspoon each of garlic, basil, and oregano and ½ teaspoon of grated Asiago cheese.

Leslie's Bread Crumbs

Here is an excellent use for day-old bread. Bread crumbs can be used immediately or stored for later. Use bread crumbs to coat vegetables, seafood, poultry, and meats before baking or frying.

Half a loaf (1 pound/455 g) day old Leslie's Sandwich Bread (page 19)
1 teaspoon garlic powder
2 teaspoons onion powder
1 teaspoon salt

Preheat oven to 250°F (120°C or gas mark ½). Cut or break day old bread into bite size pieces. Put into a food processor and make coarse crumbs. Mix in garlic powder, onion powder, and salt. Spread crumbs on a baking sheet and dry the crumbs in the oven for about 30 to 40 minutes. Turn off the heat, but keep the crumbs in the hot oven for another 2 hours or until they are dry. Remove from oven and store in an airtight container.

Yield: 3 cups
Per ¼ cup serving: 2.3g fat, 13g total carbohydrate (1.8g fiber, 11.2g net carb), 2g protein, 80 calories.

Dinner Rolls

It is possible to make great tasting gluten-free rolls. This recipe will show you how.

1 tablespoon (8.5 g) fast-acting yeast
2 tablespoons (26 g) sugar
1 cup plus 2 tablespoons (270 ml) very warm water
2½ cups (340 g) CGF Flour Mix (page 16)
1 teaspoon baking powder
1 tablespoon (9 g) xanthan gum

26

1 teaspoon salt
3 eggs at room temperature
2 tablespoons (28 g) coconut oil, melted
1 egg white
Sesame seeds

Make the dough using the first nine ingredients above according to the directions for Preparing the Dough on page 17.

Rub your hands with a little coconut oil to prevent sticking and form the dough into 12 equal size balls. Roll each ball in a little CGF Flour Mix until the outside is slightly coated. Place the dough balls on a greased baking sheet about 3 inches (7.5 cm) apart. With a sharp knife cut two slits about ¼ inch (6 mm) deep across the top of each roll. This will allow the dough to expand evenly and add a decorative touch.

Put the dough in a warm place and allow it to rise. Preheat the oven to 350°F (180°C or gas mark 4). Just before baking, brush the surface of each roll with egg white and sprinkle with sesame seeds. Bake for about 15 to 16 minutes or until tops are lightly browned.

Yield: 12 rolls
Per serving: 4.7g fat, 25.2g total carbohydrate (3.6g fiber, 21.6g net carb), 2.5g protein, 156 calories.

Gluten-Free Pizza Crust

One of the most sought after gluten-free baked products is pizza crust. Most gluten-free pizza crusts fall short. This one, however, is more like traditional pizza crust then most. The crust can be frozen, then thawed and cooked at a later time.

2 teaspoons fast-acting yeast
1 tablespoon (13 g) sugar
½ cup (120 ml) very warm water
1 cup (136 g) CGF Flour Mix (page 16)
2 teaspoons xanthan gum
½ teaspoon salt
2 eggs at room temperature
1½ cups (170 g) shredded mild or medium cheddar or Monterey Jack cheese

Make the dough using the first seven ingredients above according to the directions for Preparing the Dough on page 17. Add the shredded cheese along with the wet and dry ingredients into the mixer and mix them together. The cheese will be incorporated into the dough.

Place a sheet of parchment paper on a flat surface such as a countertop and tape it securely in place to prevent slipping. Put some coconut oil on your hands to prevent sticking, with your hands roll the dough into a ball, and place it in the center of the parchment paper. Rub a generous amount of coconut oil onto a rolling pin and roll the dough into a circle about 12 inches (30-cm) in diameter.

Remove the tape from the parchment paper, carefully lift the paper and dough together, and place them onto a baking sheet. Put the baking sheet in a warm place to allow the dough to rise until it doubles in thickness.

Preheat the oven to 350°F (180°C or gas mark 4). Bake the pizza crust for

8 to 10 minutes. At this point, the crust is only partially cooked. Remove the pizza crust from the oven. Using the parchment paper to hold the pizza crust together, carefully turn it over. Remove and discard the parchment paper. Continue cooking for another 8 minutes. If you have a pizza stone, cook the second side on the stone and shorten the cooking time to 7 minutes. We prefer to use a pizza stone when available because it cooks the crust more evenly and gives it a uniform browning.

Remove the crust from the oven. At this point, you can let the crust cool and use it later (it can be frozen) or put on the toppings and place it back in the oven to finish cooking.

Preheat the oven to 400° (200°C or gas mark 6). Bake the pizza on a pizza stone or a baking sheet. Cook for another 12 to 14 minutes (8 to 12 minutes if you use a pizza stone) or until the cheese topping is melted and the crust is a dark golden brown.

Yield: 1 (12-inch/30-cm) pizza, 8 servings
Per serving: 8.9g fat, 17.2g total carbohydrate (3.7g fiber, 13.5g net carb), 8.5g protein, 176 calories.

Single Serving Pizza Crust

The best part about the Gluten-Free Pizza Crust described above is the crispy crust along the outside edge. You can increase the amount of this part of the crust by dividing the recipe into four smaller single serving pizzas.

2 teaspoons fast-acting yeast
1 tablespoon (13 g) sugar
½ cup (120 ml) very warm water
1 cup (136 g) CGF Flour Mix (page 16)
2 teaspoons xanthan gum
½ teaspoon salt
2 eggs at room temperature
1½ cups (170 g) shredded mild or medium cheddar or Monterey Jack cheese

Make the dough using the first seven ingredients above according to the directions for Preparing the Dough on page 17. Add the shredded cheese along with the wet and dry ingredients into the mixer and mix them together. The cheese will be incorporated into the dough.

Divide the dough into four equal parts. Place four sheets of wax paper on a flat surface such as a countertop and tape them securely in place to prevent slipping. Dust each piece of wax paper with a little flour. Put some coconut oil on your hands and roll the dough out on the wax paper to about 6 inches (15cm) in diameter. Using the wax paper to help keep the dough from tearing, lift them onto a baking sheet, flip them over, and remove the wax paper. Put them in a warm place and allow them to double in thickness.

Preheat the oven to 350°F (180°C or gas mark 4). Bake the pizza crusts for 8 to 10 minutes. At this point, the crusts are only partially cooked. Remove the pizza crusts from the oven and turn them over. Continue cooking for another 8 minutes. We prefer to use a pizza stone when available because it cooks the crusts more evenly, giving a uniform browning.

Remove the crusts from the oven. At this point, you can let the crusts cool and use them later (they can be frozen) or put on the toppings and place them back in the oven to finish cooking as described below.

Preheat the oven to 400° (200°C or gas mark 6). Bake the pizzas on a pizza stone or a baking sheet. Cook for another 12 to 14 minutes

(8 to 12 minutes if you use a pizza stone) or until the cheese topping is melted and the crusts are a dark golden brown. Cool slightly on a wire rack before serving.

Yield: 4 single serving pizzas
Per serving: 8g fat, 44.8g total carbohydrate (6.2g fiber, 38,6g net carb), 6.8g protein, 274 calories.

Jalapeno Cheese Rolls

These rolls are absolutely delicious—one of our favorites!

1 tablespoon (8.5 g) fast-acting yeast
3 tablespoons (39 g) sugar
1¼ cups (300 ml) very warm water
2¼ cups (306 g) CGF Flour Mix (page 16)
¼ cup (30 g) millet flour
1 tablespoon (9 g) xanthan gum
1½ teaspoons salt
1 teaspoon baking powder
3 eggs
2 tablespoons (28 g) butter, melted
¼ cup (60 g) chopped jalapeno peppers, well drained
2 cups (200 g) cubed sharp cheddar cheese, ½ inch (6 mm) cubes
1 cup (120 g) shredded sharp cheddar cheese, for topping

Make the dough using the first ten ingredients above according to the directions for Preparing the Dough on page 17. Note that the dough in this recipe has ¼ cup (30 g) of millet flour added to the dry ingredients. After mixing the dough for 2 to 3 minutes, add jalapeno peppers and mix for additional 15 seconds or so. Mix the cheese cubes into the dough by hand.

Rub your hands with a little coconut oil to prevent sticking and form the dough into 12 equal size balls. Roll each ball in a little CGF Flour Mix to coat the outside. Place the dough balls on a greased baking sheet about 3 inches (7.5 cm) apart. With a sharp knife cut two slits about ¼ inch (6 mm) deep across the top of each roll. This will allow the dough to expand evenly and add a decorative touch.

Put the dough in a warm place and allow it to double in size. Preheat the oven to 350°F (180°C or gas mark 4). Sprinkle shredded cheese over the top of each roll. Bake in a preheated oven for about 15 to 16 minutes or until tops are lightly browned.

Yield: 12 rolls
Per serving: 13.1g fat, 26.4g total carbohydrate (3.8g fiber, 22.6g net carb), 10.7g protein, 265 calories.

Artisan Jalapeno Cheese Bread

This recipe makes excellent sandwich bread. To make the dough, follow the directions for making the Jalapeno Cheese Rolls on page 31. Once the dough is made, put a little coconut oil on your hands to prevent sticking and roll the dough into a ball. Place the ball of dough in the center of a greased baking sheet. Using a sharp knife cut three or four slits about ¼ inch (6 mm) deep across the top of the dough. This will allow the dough to expand without causing irregular rips or tears in the crust.

Put the dough in a warm place and to rise. Allow the dough to double in size. This should take about 45 minutes depending on the temperature.

Preheat the oven to 350°F (180°C or gas mark 4). Bake for 35 to 40 minutes or until the top of the loaf is a dark golden brown and the bread springs back quickly when pressed. Remove the bread from the oven and let cool on a wire rack. The bread tastes best fresh out of the oven. Store leftover bread using the storage tip on page 21.

Yield: 1 loaf (about 14 slices)
Per slice: 11.2g fat, 22.6g total carbohydrate (3.3g fiber, 19.3g net carb), 9.2g protein, 227 calories.

Rosemary Olive Rolls

1 tablespoon (8.5 g) fast-acting yeast
2 tablespoons (39 g) sugar

1 cup plus 2 tablespoons (270 ml) very warm water
2½ cups (340 g) CGF Flour Mix (page 16)
1 tablespoon (9 g) xanthan gum
1½ teaspoons salt
2 teaspoons onion powder
2 tablespoons (4.8 g) rosemary, crushed
1 teaspoon baking powder
3 eggs
3 tablespoons (28 g) extra virgin olive oil

Make the dough using the above measurements according to the directions for Preparing the Dough on page 17. Combine onion powder and rosemary with the dry ingredients when making the dough.

Rub your hands with a little olive oil to prevent sticking and form the dough into 12 equal size balls. Roll each ball in a little CGF Flour Mix to coat the outside. Place the dough balls on a greased baking sheet about 3 inches (7.5 cm) apart. With a sharp knife cut two slits about ¼ inch (6 mm) deep across the top of each roll. This will allow the dough to expand evenly and add a decorative touch.

Put the dough in a warm place and allow it double in size. Preheat the oven to 350°F (180°C or gas mark 4). With a basting brush coat the tops of the rolls with a layer extra virgin olive oil just before baking. Bake in a preheated oven for about 15 to 16 minutes or until tops are lightly browned.

Yield: 12 rolls
Per serving: 4.6g fat, 25.3g total carbohydrate (3.8g fiber, 21.5g net carb), 2.2g protein, 156 calories.

Artisan Rosemary Olive Bread

This is a great novelty and sandwich bread. To make the dough, follow the directions for making the Rosemary Olive Rolls above. Once the dough is made, rub a little coconut oil on your hands to prevent sticking and roll the dough into a ball. Place the ball of dough in the center of a greased baking sheet. Using a sharp knife cut three or four slits about ¼ inch (6 mm) deep across the top of the dough. This will allow the dough to expand without causing irregular rips or tears in the crust.

Put the dough in a warm place and to rise. Allow the dough to double in size. This should take about 45 minutes depending on the temperature.

Preheat the oven to 350°F (180°C or gas mark 4). Bake for 35 to 40 minutes or until the top of the loaf is a dark golden brown and the bread springs back quickly when pressed. Remove the bread from the oven and let cool on a wire rack. The bread tastes best fresh out of the oven. Store leftover bread using the tip on page 21.

Yield: 1 loaf (about 14 slices)
Per serving: 3.9g fat, 21.7g total carbohydrate (3.3g fiber, 18.4g net carb), 1.9g protein, 134 calories.

Seed and Nut Rolls

1 tablespoon (8.5 g) fast-acting yeast
2 tablespoons (39 g) sugar
1 cup plus 2 tablespoons (270 ml) very warm water
2½ cups (340 g) CGF Flour Mix (page 16)
1 tablespoon (9 g) xanthan gum
1½ teaspoons salt
¼ cup (34 g) sunflower seeds
½ cup (68 g) pine nuts or chopped walnuts
3 tablespoons (27 g) whole millet
1 teaspoon baking powder
3 eggs at room temperature
2 tablespoons (28 g) coconut oil, melted

Make the dough using the above measurements according to the directions for Preparing the Dough on page 17. Add sunflower seeds, nuts, and whole millet with the dry ingredients when mixing the dough.

Rub your hands with a little coconut oil to prevent sticking and form the dough into 12 equal size balls. Roll each ball in a little CGF Flour Mix to slightly coat the outside. Place the dough balls on a greased baking sheet about 3 inches (7.5 cm) apart. With a sharp knife cut two slits about ¼ inch (6 mm) deep across the top of each roll. This will allow the dough to expand evenly and add a decorative touch.

34

Put the dough in a warm place and allow it to double in size. Preheat the oven to 350°F (180°C or gas mark 4). Bake in a preheated oven for about 15 to 16 minutes or until tops are lightly browned.

Yield: 12 rolls
Per serving: 9.6g fat, 27.7g total carbohydrate (4.4g fiber, 23.3g net carb), 6.1g protein, 215 calories.

Garlic Breadsticks

Breadsticks are a great accompaniment to soups and salads. These breadsticks taste like those you get at high-end Italian restaurants.

1 tablespoon (8.5 g) fast-acting yeast
2 tablespoons (26 g) sugar
1 cup plus 2 tablespoons (270 ml) very warm water
2½ cups (340 g) CGF Flour Mix (page 16)
1 teaspoon baking powder
1 tablespoon (9 g) xanthan gum
1 teaspoon salt
3 eggs at room temperature
2 tablespoons (28 g) coconut oil, melted
3 tablespoons (42 g) butter, melted
1 teaspoon garlic powder

Make the dough using the first nine ingredients above according to the directions for Preparing the Dough on page 17.

Rub your hands with a little coconut oil, to prevent sticking, and form the dough into 12 equal size balls. Roll each ball in a little CGF Flour Mix to lightly coat the outside. Roll the balls into cylindrical shapes about 6 to 7 inches (15 to 18 cm) long. Place the dough sticks on a greased baking sheet about 2 inches (7.5 cm) apart.

Put the dough in a warm place to rise. Preheat the oven to 350°F (180°C or gas mark 4). Before baking brush the surface of each dough stick with a mixture of butter and garlic powder. Bake in a preheated oven for about 15 minutes or until light golden brown.

Yield: 12 breadsticks
Per serving: 7.6g fat, 25g total carbohydrate (3.6g fiber, 21.4g net carb), 3.9g protein, 180 calories.

Variation: You can transform these breadsticks into garlic cheese breadsticks by mixing 1 cup of shredded fresh Asiago or parmesan cheese into the dough.

Cinnamon Pull Aparts

1 tablespoon (8.5 g) fast-acting yeast
3 tablespoons (39 g) sugar
1¼ cups (300 ml) very warm water
2½ cups (340 g) CGF Flour Mix (page 16)
1 tablespoon (9 g) xanthan gum
1½ teaspoons salt
1 teaspoon baking powder
3 eggs
2 tablespoons (28 g) butter, melted
¾ cup (80 g) chopped pecans
2 teaspoons cinnamon
½ cup (100 g) granulated sugar
½ cup (75 g) lightly packed brown sugar or coconut sugar
¼ cup (55 g) butter, melted

Make the dough using the first nine ingredients above according to the directions for Preparing the Dough on page 17.

Sprinkle pecans evenly over the bottom of a well greased 11 x 7 x 2-inch (28 x 18 x 5-cm) baking dish. Combine cinnamon and granulated sugar in a bowl. Rub your hands with coconut oil to prevent sticking and form the dough into about 30 equal size balls. Roll each ball in the cinnamon sugar mix to coat the outside. Place the dough balls in the baking dish on top of the pecans. The balls should fit closely together. Put the dough-filled pan in a warm place for rising. Allow the dough to double in size. This should take about 30 to 45 minutes depending on the temperature. Preheat the oven to 350°F (180°C or gas mark 4). Mix brown sugar and ¼ cup (55 g) of melted butter together and pour over the pull aparts. Bake for 30 to 35 minutes or until the top is a dark golden brown and the bread springs back quickly when pressed. Remove from oven and let cool.

Yield: 30 pull aparts

Per serving: 5.1g fat, 16.4g total carbohydrate (1.8g fiber, 14.6g net carb), 1.8g protein, 116 calories.

Cheesy Bacon Pull Aparts

Most pull aparts are sweet. This is a delicious savory version using crumbled bacon and cheese.

1 tablespoon (8.5 g) fast-acting yeast
2 tablespoons (28 g) sugar
1¼ cups (300 ml) very warm water
2½ cups (340 g) CGF Flour Mix (page 16)
1 tablespoon (9 g) xanthan gum
1½ teaspoons salt
1 teaspoon onion powder
1 teaspoon baking powder
3 eggs
½ cup (80 g) chopped onion
2 tablespoons (28 g) butter, melted, plus some for coating the dough
1 cup (120 g) shredded mozzarella, Colby, or Monterey Jack cheese
10 strips of cooked bacon, crumbled
1 cup (120 g) shredded cheddar cheese

Make the dough using the first ten ingredients above according to the directions for Preparing the Dough on page 17.

Sprinkle the chopped onion over the bottom of a greased 11 x 7 x 2 -inch (28 x 18 x 5-cm) baking dish. Rub your hands with melted butter,

to prevent sticking, and form the dough into 15 equal size balls. Roll each ball in melted butter to coat the outside. Place the dough balls in baking dish. The balls should fit closely together but not touch.

Put the dough-filled pan in a warm place for rising. Allow the dough to double in size. This should take about 30 to 45 minutes depending on the temperature.

Preheat the oven to 350°F (180°C or gas mark 4). Sprinkle mozzarella cheese over the dough followed by the crumbled bacon and cheddar cheese. Bake for 30 to 35 minutes or until the cheese is melted and bubbly and the bread springs back quickly when pressed. Remove from the oven and let cool slightly. Serve warm.

Yield: 15 pull aparts
Per serving: 13g fat, 21.1g total carbohydrate (3.1g fiber, 18g net carb), 12g protein, 249 calories.

Marshmallow Scones

These are some of the lightest, tastiest scones you will ever eat. They are so light and delicate it's almost like eating marshmallows surrounded by a thin crispy crust. Watch out—they're addicting!

1 tablespoon (8.5 g) fast-acting yeast
¼ cup (52 g) sugar
1¼ cups (300 ml) very warm water
2 cups (270 g) CGF Flour Mix (page 16)
½ cup (64 g) tapioca flour
1 teaspoon baking powder
1 tablespoon (9 g) xanthan gum
1½ teaspoons salt
3 eggs at room temperature
2 tablespoons (28 g) coconut oil, melted

Make the dough using the ingredients above according to the directions for Preparing the Dough on page 17.

Rub your hands with a little coconut oil to prevent sticking and form the dough into 12 equal size balls. Roll each ball in CGF Flour Mix to coat the outside. Place the dough balls on a greased baking sheet about 2 inches (5 cm) apart. Flatten the balls so that they are about ¼ inch (6 mm) thick.

Put the dough in a warm place to rise until doubled in size. Preheat coconut oil in a deep fryer to 350°F (180°C). If you don't have a deep fryer, you can use a large saucepan filled with coconut oil about 2 inches

(5 cm) deep over medium heat. Cook the dough until the scones are lightly browned. Remove and let cool. Top with butter, honey, jam, or syrup.

Yield: 12 scones
Per serving: 6.5g fat, 27.4g total carbohydrate (3.4g fiber, 24g net carb), 3.7g protein, 184 calories.

Scone Breakfast Sandwich

Scones don't have to be sweet. We like to cut them in half like an English muffin and serve them with fried eggs or with a combination of eggs, cheese, and ham. They make an excellent alternative to an Egg McMuffin. We call them Scone Breakfast Sandwiches.

To make these sandwiches follow the directions for making Marshmallow Scones above. After cooking the scones, cut them in half like you would a bun or roll. Add a slice of cheese, a slice of ham, and an egg. You can use fried or scrambled eggs.

Scones can also function like rolls to make other types of sandwiches. Try chicken, turkey, avocado and tomato, tuna fish, and other sandwich fillings and serve for lunch or dinner.

Yield: 12 scones
Per serving: varies depending on filling.

Donut Holes

Most donuts are made with wheat flour and cooked in hydrogenated oil. These donut holes are wheat-free and gluten-free and cooked in healthy coconut oil, making them a much better option for health-conscious individuals.

Dough

1 tablespoon (8.5 g) fast-acting yeast
2 tablespoons (26 g) sugar, to be combined with yeast
1¼ cups (300 ml) very warm water
2¼ cups (300 g) CGF Flour Mix (page 16)
¼ cup (32 g) tapioca flour
¾ cup (150 g) sugar, to be mixed with flour
1 teaspoon baking powder
1 tablespoon (9 g) xanthan gum
1½ teaspoons salt
1 tablespoon (7 g) cinnamon
2 teaspoons nutmeg
3 eggs at room temperature
2 tablespoons (28 g) coconut oil, melted
Coconut oil for frying

Make the dough using the first 13 ingredients above according to the directions for Preparing the Dough on page 17. Note that 2 tablespoons (26 g) of sugar will be used in activating the yeast and another ¾ cup (150 g) of sugar will be added to the dough before mixing.

Rub your hands with a little coconut oil, to prevent sticking, and form the dough into 24 equal size balls. Roll each ball in CGF Flour Mix to coat the outside. Place the dough balls on a greased baking sheet about 2 inches (5 cm) apart.

Put the dough in a warm place to rise and double in size. Preheat coconut oil in a deep fryer to 350°F (180°C). If you don't have a deep fryer you can use a large saucepan filled with coconut oil about 2 inches (5 cm) deep on medium heat. Cook the dough until the donut holes are browned (about 1½ minutes), turn and cook the other side. Remove and let cool on a plate covered with a paper towel. Dust with powdered sugar or top with donut glaze before serving.

Donut Glaze
This is a basic donut glaze. For a maple glaze substitute ¼ teaspoon of maple extract for the vanilla.

2 tablespoons (28 ml) cream
¼ teaspoon vanilla extract
1 cup (120 g) powdered sugar

Combine cream and vanilla and gradually blend in powdered sugar. Add additional cream if needed to reach desired consistency. Immediately cover the tops of the donut holes with the soft glaze one at a time and set aside to allow the glaze to harden.

Yield: 24 donut holes
Per serving: 3g fat, 23.8g total carbohydrate (1.8g fiber, 22g net carb), 1.8g protein, 126 calories.

Baked Donut Holes
Donuts don't have to be deep fried. They also taste delicious baked. Follow the directions for making donut holes above until they are ready to cook. Then preheat the oven to 350°F (180°C or gas mark 4). Cook for 15 minutes. Remove from oven and let cool. Dust with powdered sugar or dip into a donut glaze before serving.

Yield: 24 donut holes
Per serving: 2.4g fat, 23.8g total carbohydrate (1.8g fiber, 22g net carb), 1.8g protein, 121 calories.

Cinnamon Sticks

1 tablespoon (8.5 g) fast-acting yeast
¼ cup (52 g) sugar
1¼ cups (300 ml) very warm water
2½ cups (340 g) CGF Flour Mix (page 16)
1 teaspoon baking powder

1 tablespoon (9 g) xanthan gum
1½ teaspoons salt
3 eggs at room temperature
2 tablespoons (28 g) coconut oil, melted
Powdered sugar and cinnamon for coating

Make the dough using the first 10 ingredients above according to the directions for Preparing the Dough on page 17.

Rub your hands with a little coconut oil to prevent sticking and form the dough into egg-size balls. Roll each ball in CGF flour until they are about 4 to 5 inches (10 to 13 cm) long. Place the dough sticks on a greased baking sheet about 2 inches (5 cm) apart.

Put the dough in a warm place to rise. Preheat coconut oil in deep fryer to 350°F (180°C). If you don't have a deep fryer you can use a large sauce pan filled with about 2 inches (5 cm) of coconut oil. Cook the dough until lightly browned. Remove and let cool. Dust with powdered sugar and cinnamon.

Yields: 15 to 18 cinnamon sticks
Per serving: 3.1g fat, 18.1g total carbohydrate (2.4g fiber, 15.7g net carb), 2.6g protein, 110 calories.

Sweet Kolaches

When we moved to Houston, Texas we were introduced to a pastry called a kolache, which is local favorite. Kolaches are soft pastries containing a filling that can be either sweet or savory. Here we provide a basic kolache recipe with a choice of three sweet fillings—pineapple, apple, and pecan. Each filling recipe makes enough for 12 kolaches.

Pineapple Filling

1 cup (165 g) crushed pineapple
¼ cup (38 g) loosely packed brown sugar or coconut sugar
2½ teaspoons cornstarch
1 tablespoon (14 g) butter
½ teaspoon vanilla extract

In a small saucepan over medium heat cook pineapple, brown sugar, cornstarch, and butter until the mixture thickens slightly. Remove from heat and add vanilla extract. Let cool.

Apple Filling

1 tart apple, chopped
½ cup (75 g) loosely packed brown sugar or coconut sugar
¼ cup (60 ml) water
2 teaspoons cornstarch
1 tablespoon (14 g) butter
½ teaspoon cinnamon

In a small saucepan over medium heat cook apple, brown sugar, water, cornstarch, and butter until the mixture thickens. Remove from heat and add cinnamon. Let cool.

Pecan Filling

1 egg
½ cup (75 g) loosely packed brown sugar or coconut sugar
2 tablespoons (28 g) butter, melted
2 tablespoons (19 g) tapioca flour or cornstarch
¼ teaspoon vanilla extract
½ cup (55 g) finely chopped pecans
Dash salt

In a bowl, blend together egg, sugar, butter, tapioca flour, vanilla extract, pecans and salt.

Dough

1 tablespoon (8.5 g) fast-acting yeast
¼ cup (52 g) sugar

1¼ cups (300 ml) very warm water
2½ cups (340 g) CGF Flour Mix (page 16)
1 teaspoon baking powder
1 tablespoon (9 g) xanthan gum
1½ teaspoons salt
3 eggs at room temperature
2 tablespoons (28 g) coconut oil, melted
Powdered sugar for coating

Make the dough using the first nine ingredients above according to the directions for Preparing the Dough on page 17.

Rub your hands with a little coconut oil to prevent sticking and form the dough into 12 equal size balls. Roll each ball in CGF Flour Mix to coat the outside. Place the dough balls on a greased baking sheet about 2 inches (5 cm) apart. Using a spoon, make a depression in the center of each dough ball for the filling. Fill each depression with about 1 tablespoon (20 g) of filling.

Put the dough in a warm place and allow it to double in size. Preheat the oven to 350°F (180°C or gas mark 4). Bake for about 14 to 15 minutes or until the crusts are golden brown. Remove from oven and put on a cooling rack. Dust with powdered sugar.

Yield: 12 kolaches
Per serving: 6.2g fat, 35.9g total carbohydrate (4g fiber, 31.9g net carb), 4g protein, 205 calories.

Sausage Kolache

This is one of the most popular savory kolaches. It is basically a link sausage wrapped in a bread coating.

1 tablespoon (8.5 g) fast-acting yeast
2 tablespoons (26 g) sugar
1¼ cups (300 ml) very warm water
2½ cups (340 g) CGF Flour Mix (page 16)
1 teaspoon baking powder
1 tablespoon (9 g) xanthan gum
1½ teaspoons salt

2 teaspoons onion powder
3 eggs
2 tablespoons (28 g) butter, melted
12 link sausages, cooked

Make the dough using the first nine ingredients above according to the directions for Preparing the Dough on page 17.
Rub your hands with a little coconut oil to prevent sticking and form the dough into 12 equal size balls. Roll each ball in CGF Flour Mix to coat the outside. Place the dough balls on a greased baking sheet and flatten. Wrap each flattened dough ball around one sausage link. Place wrapped links about 2 inches (5 cm) apart.
Put the dough in a warm place to rise. Preheat the oven to 350°F (180°C or gas mark 4). Bake for 15 to 16 minutes or until crusts are golden brown. Remove from oven and put on a cooling rack.

Yield: 12 kolaches
Per serving: 8.4g fat, 25.4g total carbohydrate (3.6g fiber, 21.8g net carb), 6.5g protein, 201 calories.

Navajo Fry Bread

During our college days we discovered Navajo tacos—fry bread smothered in chili beans, cheese, lettuce, sliced tomatoes, and avocado. They were delicious. You can make your own Navajo tacos with this fry bread recipe. Fry bread isn't just for Navajo tacos, however. It makes a great accompaniment to a bowl of pork and beans, chili, stew, or soup. It can also be used like toast or sliced bread to make open-faced sandwiches.

1 tablespoon (8.5 g) fast-acting yeast
2 tablespoons (26 g) sugar
1¼ cups (300 ml) very warm water
2¼ cups (306 g) CGF Flour Mix (page 16)
¼ cup (30 g) millet flour
1 teaspoon baking powder
1 tablespoon (9 g) xanthan gum
1½ teaspoons salt

3 eggs at room temperature
2 tablespoons (28 g) coconut oil, melted

Make the dough using the ingredients above according to the directions for Preparing the Dough on page 17. Note that millet flour is added to the dry ingredients.

Rub your hands with a little coconut oil to prevent sticking and form the dough into 8 equal size balls. Roll each ball in CGF Flour Mix to coat the outside. Place the dough balls on a greased baking sheet and flatten them so that they are no more than ¼ inch (6 mm) thick.

Put the dough in a warm place to rise. Preheat coconut oil in a deep fryer to 350°F (180°C). If you don't have a deep fryer you can use a large saucepan filled with about 2 inches (5 cm) of coconut oil. Cook the dough until the bread is browned. Remove and let cool.

Yield: 8 servings
Per serving: 2.4g fat, 36.9g total carbohydrate (5.3g fiber, 31.6g net carb), 5.9g protein, 245 calories.

Hamburger and Hot Dog Buns

The trick to making good gluten-free hamburger and hot dog buns is getting the dimensions right. These buns are slightly thinner than commercial rolls, which is a plus because most commercial products have way too much bread, especially hot dog buns. You usually get much more bun than you do meat. Not here. These buns provide just enough to hold the meat without overwhelming it.

1 tablespoon (8.5 g) fast-acting yeast
2 tablespoons (26 g) sugar
1 cup plus 2 tablespoons (270 ml) very warm water
2½ cups (340 g) CGF Flour Mix (page 16)
1 teaspoon baking powder
1 tablespoon (9 g) xanthan gum
1 teaspoon salt
3 eggs at room temperature
2 tablespoons (28 g) coconut oil, melted

Make the dough using the ingredients above according to the directions for Preparing the Dough on page 17.

Rub your hands with a little coconut oil to prevent sticking and form the dough into 8 equal size balls. Roll each ball in a little CGF Flour Mix to coat the outside.

To make the hamburger buns, place the dough balls on a greased baking sheet and flatten them so that they are about 4 inches (10 cm) in diameter and about ½ to ¾ inch (1 to 2 cm) thick. With a sharp knife cut a cross on the top of each roll about ¼ inch (6 mm) deep. This will allow the dough to expand evenly and add a decorative touch.

Flatten and shape the dough on a baking sheet.

After the dough has risen it is ready to be placed it in the oven.

These hamburger and hot dog buns provide just the right amount of bun for the meat.

To make the hot dog buns, roll each dough ball between your hands to produce a log shape about 5 to 5½ inches (13 to 14 cm) long. Place the dough on the baking sheet and flatten to ½ inch (1 cm) thick. After flattening, the dough should be about 2 to 2½ inches (5 to 6 cm) wide. Cut a slit lengthwise down the center of each bun about ¼ inch (6 mm) deep.

Put the dough in a warm place and allow it to double in size. Preheat the oven to 350°F (180°C or gas mark 4). Bake for about 18 minutes or until the tops are lightly browned. Remove from the oven and let cool. Slice each bun in half and fill with meat and condiments. Tastes best right out of the oven.

Yield: 8 buns
Per bun: 6.9g fat, 37.3g total carbohydrate (5.4g fiber, 31.9g net carb), 5.8g protein, 232 calories.

Cinnamon Rolls

Finally, a gluten-free cinnamon roll that tastes as good as Mother used to make! This recipe takes a little longer to prepare than most of the others in this book because the dough has to be flattened out, filled, rolled up, and cut before rising, but it is well worth it.

Dough

1 tablespoon (8.5 g) fast-acting yeast
¼ cup (52 g) sugar
1 cup plus 2 tablespoons (270 ml) very warm water
2½ cups (340 g) CGF Flour Mix (page 16)
1 teaspoon baking powder
1 tablespoon (9 g) xanthan gum
1½ teaspoons salt
3 eggs
2 tablespoons (28 g) butter, melted

Filling

2 tablespoons (28 g) butter, melted
¾ cup (170 g) firmly packed brown sugar
1 tablespoon (8 g) cinnamon
½ cup (75 g) raisins
½ cup (55 g) chopped pecans or walnuts

White Icing

¼ teaspoon vanilla extract
2 tablespoons (30 ml) cream or coconut milk
1 cup (120 g) powdered sugar

Make the dough using the first nine ingredients above according to the directions for Preparing the Dough on page 17.

Place a 16 inch (40 cm) sheet of parchment paper on a flat surface such as a countertop and tape it securely in place

50

to prevent slipping. Rub your hands and the surface of the parchment paper with a little coconut oil to prevent sticking. Form the dough into two equal size balls. Roll one ball in a little CGF flour and shape it into a log about 8 inches (20 cm) long, then place it in the center of the parchment paper. Rub a generous amount of coconut oil onto a rolling pin to prevent sticking, and roll out the dough on the parchment paper into a rectangle shape about 12 inches (30 cm) in length and 9 inches (23 cm) in width.

The dough is now ready for the filling. The filling ingredients will be divided in half. Using a basting brush, apply 1 tablespoon (14 g) of melted butter in an even layer on the dough. Sprinkle on half of the brown sugar, cinnamon, raisins, and nuts. With the aid of the parchment paper, carefully roll the dough into a log shape. Cut the log into 1½ to 2 inch (3 to 5cm) thick segments. Repeat with the second ball of dough. Arrange the rolls evenly in a greased 11 x 7 x 2-inch (28 x 18 x 5-cm) baking dish.

Put the dish in a warm place and allow the dough to double in size. Preheat oven to 350°F (180°C or gas mark 4). Bake for

25 minutes. Remove from the oven and let cool.

To make the icing, combine vanilla extract with cream. Stir in sugar a little at a time and blend until smooth. Adjust the amount of cream you use to obtain the desired consistency. The icing will start to harden if left to stand, so immediately drizzle it over the tops of the cinnamon rolls while it is still soft.

Yields: about 18 rolls
Per serving: 6.4g fat, 37.8g total carbohydrate (2.9g fiber, 34.9g net carb), 3.1g protein, 216 calories.

Gourmet Tortillas

Gluten-free tortillas are one of those items that are hard to find. Our version is actually better than standard tortillas, which is why we call them gourmet tortillas. They are softer and lighter than traditional flour tortillas.

2 teaspoons fast-acting yeast
1 tablespoon (13 g) sugar
½ cup (120 ml) very warm water
1 cup (136 g) CGF Flour Mix (page 16)
1 tablespoon (7 g) millet flour

2 teaspoons xanthan gum
½ teaspoon salt
2 eggs at room temperature
1 tablespoon (14 g) coconut oil, melted

Make the dough using the ingredients above according to the directions for Preparing the Dough on page 17.

Rub your hands with a little coconut oil to prevent sticking and form the dough into 6 equal size balls. Roll each ball in a little CGF Flour Mix to slightly coat the outside. Roll out each tortilla on a separate sheet of parchment paper until very thin, about ⅛ inch (3 mm). Keep in mind that when the dough rises it will double in thickness. Cut off excess parchment paper around each tortilla and place the tortilla together with its underlying layer of parchment paper on a baking sheet.

Put the dough in a warm place to allow it to rise. Preheat the oven to 350°F (180°C or gas mark 4). Bake for 10 minutes. Remove from the oven, peel off parchment paper, and let cool. Fill the tortillas with refried beans, grilled meat and vegetables, or ham and eggs, then wrap and enjoy.

Yield: 6 tortillas
Per serving: 5g fat, 22.7g total carbohydrate (3.9g fiber, 18.8g net carb), 5.3g protein, 152 calories.

Flatbread

This gluten-free flatbread can be eaten like a slice of bread. It tastes fantastic right out of the oven with a dab of butter and jam. It also makes excellent open faced sandwiches or can be used as the crust for an individual serving of pizza. For pizza, simply add toppings to the cooked flatbread and bake it in the oven until the cheese is melted.

2 teaspoons fast-acting yeast
1 tablespoon (13 g) sugar
½ cup (120 ml) very warm water
1 cup (136 g) CGF Flour Mix (page 16)
2 teaspoons xanthan gum
½ teaspoon salt
2 eggs at room temperature
1 tablespoon (14 g) coconut oil, melted

Make the dough using the ingredients above according to the directions for Preparing the Dough on page 17.

Rub your hands with a little coconut oil to prevent sticking and form the dough into 4 equal size balls. Roll each ball in a little CGF Flour Mix to coat the outside. Evenly space the dough balls on a baking sheet. With a rolling pin flatten out each dough ball until it is about 5 to 6 inches (13 to 15 cm) in diameter and no more than ¼ inch (6 mm) thick.

Put the dough in a warm place to allow it to rise. Preheat the oven to 350°F (180°C or gas mark 4). Bake for 10 minutes. Flip and bake another 2 to 3 minutes.

Yield: 4
Per serving: 7.4g fat, 26.2g total carbohydrate (5.7g fiber, 27.1g net carb), 7.7g protein, 221 calories.

3

Pancakes and Waffles

This chapter contains a variety of pancakes and waffles along with a few other traditional breakfast recipes such as crepes and French toast. Some of the recipes use only coconut flour, but most use the CGF Flour Mix. You will find a variety of pancake recipes ranging from sweet treats such as peanut butter and banana, blueberry, cherry, and pineapple, to more savory cakes like cheese, sausage, corn and pepper, and mushroom and onion, plus a few novelty recipes such as our pumpkin and protein pancakes. CGF Flour Mix makes extraordinary waffles that are deliciously crisp on the outside but mouthwateringly soft on the inside. Waffle recipes range from apple to ham and cheese. Also included are waffle recipes that can be used as a pizza crust, eaten like toast, or made into sandwiches. If you miss the standard wheat toast, gluten-free waffle toast makes a surprisingly good replacement.

Coconut Flour Pancakes

This is a basic gluten-free coconut flour pancake recipe. The only flour used in this recipe is coconut flour.

2 eggs
2 tablespoons (30 ml) whole milk or coconut milk
2½ tablespoons (35 g) coconut oil or butter, melted
1 teaspoon sugar
¼ teaspoon vanilla extract
⅛ teaspoon salt
2 tablespoons (16 g) coconut flour, sifted
⅛ teaspoon baking powder
Coconut oil for frying

Blend together, eggs, milk, sugar, vanilla extract, and salt. Combine coconut flour and baking powder and whisk into the batter. Heat the oil in a skillet. When a drop of cold water will dance on the skillet, begin cooking the pancakes. Spoon batter onto hot skillet, making pancakes 3 to 4 inches (8 to 10 cm) in diameter. Batter will be thick but will thin out when cooking. Cook until the pancake is strong enough to flip and cook the other side. Serve hot with syrup or jam.

Yield: 6 pancakes
Per serving: 7.8g fat, 2.4g total carbohydrate (0.8g fiber, 1.6g net carb), 2.3g protein, 87 calories.

Peanut Butter and Banana Pancakes

2 eggs
2 tablespoons (30 ml) whole milk or cream
1 teaspoon sugar
⅛ teaspoon salt
3 tablespoons (48 g) crunchy peanut butter
1 tablespoon (14 g) coconut oil, melted
2 tablespoons (16 g) coconut flour
¼ teaspoon baking powder
1 medium banana
Coconut oil for frying

Blend together eggs, milk or cream, sugar, and salt. Mix in peanut butter and coconut oil. Combine coconut flour and baking powder and whisk into wet mixture. Cut banana into ⅛-inch (3 mm) thick slices. Cut each slice in half. Fold banana slices into batter. Batter will be thick. Put skillet on medium heat with a little coconut oil. Spoon batter onto the hot skillet. Flatten out each pancake to about 3 to 4 inches (8 to 10 cm) in diameter. Cook until the pancake is strong enough to flip and cook the other side. Serve as is or add a topping of your choice.

Yield: 6 pancakes
Per serving: 8.4g fat, 8.4g total carbohydrate (1.8g fiber, 22g net carb), 4.6g protein, 121 calories.

Gluten-Free Pancakes
This recipe uses the CGF Flour Mix.

2 eggs
½ cup (120 ml) milk
⅛ teaspoon salt
1 teaspoon coconut oil, melted
¼ teaspoon vanilla extract
1 teaspoon sugar
½ cup plus 2 tablespoons (86 g) CGF Flour Mix (page 16)
½ teaspoon baking powder
Coconut oil for frying

Blend together eggs, milk, salt, coconut oil, vanilla extract, and sugar. Combine CGF flour with baking powder and whisk into wet ingredients until smooth. Heat coconut oil in a skillet. When a drop of cold water dances on the skillet, begin cooking the pancakes. Spoon batter onto the hot skillet, making pancakes about 4 inches (10 cm) in diameter. When the bubbles on top of the pancake begin to break, flip and cook the other side. Serve topped with syrup or jam.

Yield: 6 pancakes
Per serving: 3.1g fat, 11.5g total carbohydrate (1.4g fiber, 10.1g net carb), 3g protein, 85 calories.

Blueberry Pancakes

2 eggs
½ cup (120 ml) milk
⅛ teaspoon salt
1 teaspoon coconut oil, melted
¼ teaspoon almond extract
1 teaspoon sugar
⅔ cup (90 g) CGF Flour Mix (page 16)
½ teaspoon baking powder
½ cup (75 g) fresh blueberries, washed and dried
Coconut oil for frying

Blend together eggs, milk, salt, coconut oil, almond extract, and sugar. Combine CGF flour with baking powder and whisk into wet ingredients until smooth. Fold in fresh blueberries. Heat coconut oil in a skillet. Spoon batter onto the hot skillet, making pancakes about 4 inches (10 cm) in diameter. Serve with syrup, honey, or topping of your choice.

Yield: 6 pancakes
Per serving: 3.5g fat, 15g total carbohydrate (1.5g fiber, 13.5g net carb), 3.7g protein, 107 calories.

Cherry Pancakes

2 eggs
½ cup (120 ml) milk
⅛ teaspoon salt
1 teaspoon coconut oil, melted
¼ teaspoon almond extract
1 teaspoon sugar
½ cup plus 2 tablespoons (86 g) CGF Flour Mix (page 16)
½ teaspoon baking powder
½ cup (72 g) dried cherries
Coconut oil for frying

Blend together eggs, milk, salt, coconut oil, vanilla extract, and sugar. Combine CGF flour with baking powder and whisk into wet ingredients until smooth. Fold in dried cherries. Heat coconut oil in a skillet. Spoon batter onto the hot skillet, making pancakes about 4 inches (10 cm) in diameter. Serve with syrup, honey, or topping of your choice.

Yield: 6 pancakes
Per serving: 6g fat, 15.6g total carbohydrate (1.4g fiber, 14.2g net carb), 5.5g protein, 141 calories.

Pineapple Pancakes

2 eggs
¼ cup (60 ml) milk
⅛ teaspoon salt
¼ teaspoon orange extract
1 teaspoon coconut oil, melted
¼ cup (40 g) crushed pineapple
½ cup (68 g) CGF Flour Mix (page 16)
½ teaspoon baking powder
Coconut oil for frying

Blend together eggs, milk, salt, orange extract, and coconut oil. Stir in crushed pineapple. Combine CGF flour with baking powder and whisk into wet ingredients until smooth. Heat coconut oil in a skillet. Spoon batter onto the hot skillet, making pancakes about 4 inches (10 cm) in diameter. Serve with topping of your choice.

Yield: 6 pancakes
Per serving: 3.1g fat, 9.9g total carbohydrate (1.1g fiber, 8.8g net carb), 3g protein, 79 calories.

Variation: For a truly tropical pancake, add ¼ cup (20 g) of flaked coconut to the batter before cooking.

Protein Pancakes

These high protein pancakes turn a beautiful golden color when cooked and take on a slight crispness.

2 eggs
¼ cup (60 ml) milk
⅛ teaspoon salt
1 teaspoon coconut oil, melted
3 tablespoons (42 g) cottage cheese
½ cup (48 g) vanilla whey protein powder
½ cup (68 g) CGF Flour Mix (page 16)
½ teaspoon baking powder
Coconut oil for frying

Blend together eggs, milk, salt, and coconut oil. Stir in cottage cheese and whey powder. Combine CGF flour with baking powder and whisk into wet ingredients until smooth. Heat coconut oil in a skillet. Spoon batter onto the hot skillet, making pancakes about 4½ inches (12 cm) in diameter. Serve with topping of your choice.

Yield: 6 pancakes
Per serving: 3.7g fat, 10.2g total carbohydrate (1.1g fiber, 9.1g net carb), 9.3g protein, 131 calories.

Pumpkin Spice Pancakes

2 eggs
¼ cup (60 ml) milk
¼ teaspoon salt
½ teaspoon cinnamon
¼ teaspoon nutmeg
⅛ teaspoon ginger
⅛ teaspoon cloves
¼ teaspoon vanilla extract
1 tablespoon (13 g) sugar
2 tablespoons (28 g) butter, melted

½ cup (122 g) mashed pumpkin
½ cup (68 g) CGF Flour Mix (page 16)
½ teaspoon baking powder
Coconut oil for frying

Blend together eggs, milk, salt, cinnamon, nutmeg, ginger, cloves, vanilla extract, sugar, butter, and pumpkin. Combine CGF flour with baking powder and whisk into wet ingredients until smooth. Heat coconut oil in a skillet. Spoon batter onto the hot skillet, making pancakes about 3 to 4 inches (10 cm) in diameter. Goes well topped with maple syrup or honey.

Yield: 6 pancakes
Per serving: 6.2g fat, 12.9g total carbohydrate (1.8g fiber, 11.1g net carb), 3.3g protein, 118 calories.

Cheese Pancakes

Not all pancakes need to be sweet or be served with sweet toppings. These savory pancakes are some of our favorites. Cook them with plenty of coconut oil to prevent sticking and to give them a slight crispness.

2 eggs
⅛ teaspoon salt
½ teaspoon onion powder
2 tablespoons (28 g) butter, melted
3 tablespoons (45 ml) water
½ cup (68 g) CGF Flour Mix (page 16)
½ teaspoon baking powder
¾ cup (90 g) shredded sharp cheddar cheese
Coconut oil for frying

Blend together eggs, salt, onion powder, butter, and water. Combine CGF flour with baking powder and whisk into wet ingredients until smooth. Stir in cheese. Heat coconut oil in a skillet. Spoon batter onto hot skillet, making pancakes about 4 inches (10 cm) in diameter. These pancakes taste great as is, but if you like you can add butter or sour cream.

Yield: 6 pancakes
Per serving: 10.8g fat, 8.9g total carbohydrate (1.1g fiber, 7.8g net carb), 6.5g protein, 158 calories.

Variation: You can kick up the flavor of these pancakes by adding 1 tablespoon of diced jalapeno peppers.

Sausage Pancakes

This is another one of our all-time favorite pancakes. For spicier pancakes use sausage seasoned with hot peppers.

¼ pound (115 g) cooked pork or turkey sausage
2 eggs
¼ teaspoon salt
½ teaspoon onion powder
2 tablespoons (28 g) butter, melted
½ cup (60 ml) water
½ cup (68 g) CGF Flour Mix (page 16)
½ teaspoon baking powder
¾ cup (90 g) shredded sharp cheddar cheese
Coconut oil for frying

Brown sausage in a skillet and set aside to cool. In a bowl, blend together eggs, salt, onion powder, butter, and water. Combine CGF flour with baking powder and whisk into wet ingredients until smooth. Stir in cheese and cooked sausage. Heat coconut oil in a skillet. Spoon batter onto hot skillet, making pancakes about 4 inches (10 cm) in diameter. Use plenty of coconut oil for frying to prevent sticking.

Yield: 6 pancakes
Per serving: 16.2g fat, 8.9g total carbohydrate (1.1g fiber, 7.8g net carb), 10.2g protein, 223 calories.

Corn and Pepper Pancakes

These tasty pancakes make a great main course for breakfast or a nice side dish for dinner. Serve in place of potatoes or corn. The millet flour gives these pancakes a little added flavor. If you don't have millet flour handy, you can increase CGF Flour Mix by 2 tablespoons (18 g).

½ cup (80 g) finely chopped onion
¼ cup (38 g) finely chopped red bell pepper
3 tablespoons (42 g) butter
½ cup (68 g) well drained whole kernel corn
2 eggs
½ teaspoon salt
½ teaspoon onion powder
½ cup (60 ml) water
½ cup (68 g) CGF Flour Mix (page 16)
2 tablespoons (15 g) millet flour
½ teaspoon baking powder
¾ cup (90 g) shredded sharp cheddar cheese
8 strips cooked bacon, crumbled
Bacon grease for frying

Sauté onions and bell pepper in butter until the vegetables are soft. Add corn, cook for another minute, remove from heat, and let cool. In a bowl, blend together eggs, salt, onion powder, and water. Combine CGF flour and millet flour with baking powder and whisk into wet ingredients until smooth. Stir in bacon and cooked vegetables, including the butter and juices. Heat bacon grease in a skillet. Spoon batter onto hot skillet, making pancakes about 4 inches (10 cm) in diameter.

Yield: 8 pancakes
Per serving: 17.6g fat, 11.2g total carbohydrate (1.5g fiber, 9.7g net carb), 11.5g protein, 254 calories.

Mushroom and Onion Pancakes

1 cup (160 g) finely chopped onion
3 tablespoons (42 g) butter
2 cups (140 g) chopped mushrooms
2 eggs
½ teaspoon salt

64

½ teaspoon onion powder
½ cup plus 1 tablespoon (75 ml) water
½ cup (68 g) CGF Flour Mix (page 16)
½ teaspoon baking powder
½ cup (58 g) shredded fresh Asiago or parmesan cheese
Coconut oil for frying

Sauté onions in butter for about two minutes. Add mushrooms and continue cooking until the vegetables are soft. Remove from heat and let cool. In a bowl, blend together eggs, salt, onion powder, and water. Combine CGF flour with baking powder and whisk into wet ingredients until smooth. Stir in cheese and cooked vegetables, including the butter and juices. Spoon batter onto hot skillet, making pancakes about 4 inches (10 cm) in diameter.

Yield: 8 pancakes
Per serving: 7.9g fat, 9g total carbohydrate (1.3g fiber, 7.7g net carb), 4.6g protein, 124 calories.

Gluten-Free Crepes
Crepes are basically very thin pancakes wrapped around a sweet or savory filling.

2 eggs
½ cup (120 ml) milk
⅛ teaspoon salt
¼ teaspoon vanilla extract
1 tablespoon (13 g) sugar
1 teaspoon coconut oil, melted
3 tablespoons (27 g) CGF Flour Mix (page 16)
¼ teaspoon baking powder
Coconut oil for frying

Blend together eggs, milk, salt, vanilla extract, sugar, and coconut oil. Combine CGF flour with baking powder and whisk into wet ingredients until smooth. Batter will be very thin. Heat a small amount of coconut oil in a 6-inch (15-cm) skillet. Spoon ¼ cup (65 ml) of batter into the center of the skillet, tipping it back and forth so the batter just coats the bottom of the pan. The crepe will be very thin. Brown lightly on one side, then carefully turn and brown the other side. Spread with jam, honey, marmalade, or fruit or simply drizzle with melted butter and dust with powdered sugar. Roll up and top with whipped cream if desired. For savory crepes fill with creamed or chopped meat, seafood, or vegetables.

Yield: 4 crepes
Per serving: 4.7g fat, 17.8g total carbohydrate (1.7g fiber, 16.1g net carb), 5.1g protein, 134 calories.

Best Ever Gluten-Free Waffles

These are the best tasting gluten-free waffles you will probably ever eat! They are light, crispy, and taste great. You can make several and freeze the leftovers to reheat for a quick and easy breakfast on another day. Just pull them out of the freezer 10 minutes before cooking. To reheat, simply stick them onto a hot waffle iron for a couple of minutes. Day-old unfrozen waffles can be reheated the same way.

2 eggs
1 cup (240 ml) water
¼ teaspoon salt
2 teaspoons coconut oil, melted
¼ teaspoon vanilla extract
1 tablespoon (13 g) sugar
1 cup (136 g) CGF Flour Mix (page 16)
1 teaspoon baking powder

Blend together eggs, water, salt, coconut oil, vanilla extract, and sugar. Combine CGF flour with baking powder and whisk into wet ingredients until smooth. Spoon batter onto hot waffle maker and cook for about 6 minutes or until waffles are a light golden tan. Serve topped with fruit, whipped cream, syrup, or jam.

Yield: about 6 waffles
Per serving: 3.5g fat, 10.6g total carbohydrate (1.1g fiber, 9.5g net carb), 2.7g protein, 84 calories.

66

Best Ever Gluten-Free Waffle

Sandwich Waffles

These are one of our favorite recipes because they taste so good and are extraordinarily versatile. They can be used much like any sandwich bread. Add a little butter as they come out of the waffle iron and they make delicious crispy toast. Serve them topped with fried eggs, ham, or bacon, or make a sandwich out of them just as you would ordinary toast. You can even use them as breakfast waffles topped with syrup, fruit, and whipped cream.

Make extra and use them as sandwich bread for lunch or dinner. When stored in a plastic bag, the waffles soften up, becoming ideal sandwich bread. Don't close the bag completely; leave a small opening to allow a little air in to prevent them from becoming too soft. Use them to make peanut butter and jelly, ham and cheese, chicken and avocado, or just about any type of sandwich you like.

Day-old waffles can be toasted in a regular toaster, but they burn easily so keep them in only a minute or two. We prefer to toast them by putting them in a hot waffle iron for a couple of minutes.

2 eggs
1 cup (240 ml) water
¼ teaspoon salt
2 tablespoons (28 g) butter, melted
1 cup (136 g) CGF Flour Mix (page 16)
1 teaspoon baking powder

Blend together eggs, water, salt, and butter. Combine CGF flour with baking powder and whisk into wet ingredients until smooth. Spoon batter onto hot waffle maker and cook for about 6 minutes or until waffles are a light golden tan.

Yield: about 6 waffles
Per serving: 3.7g fat, 17.5g total carbohydrate (2.3g fiber, 15.2g net carb), 3.6g protein, 119 calories.

Apple Waffles

2 eggs
¾ cup (180 ml) water
¼ teaspoon salt
2 tablespoons (26 g) sugar
½ teaspoon almond extract
2 tablespoons (28 g) butter, melted
1 cup (136 g) CGF Flour Mix (page 16)
1 teaspoon baking powder
1 cup (150 g) diced tart apple
½ cup (60 g) chopped walnut
½ cup (60 g) raisins

Blend together eggs, water, salt, sugar, almond extract, and butter. Combine CGF flour with baking powder and whisk into wet ingredients until smooth. Stir in apple, walnuts, and raisins. Spoon batter onto hot waffle maker and cook for about 6 minutes or until waffles are a golden brown. Eat as is or serve with syrup.

Yield: about 6 waffles

Per serving: 12.3g fat, 34.1g total carbohydrate (3.9g fiber, 30.2g net carb), 6.4g protein, 263 calories.

Garlic Waffles

2 eggs
1 cup (240 ml) water
¼ teaspoon salt
1 teaspoon onion powder
¼ cup (56 g) butter, melted
1 cup (136 g) CGF Flour Mix (page 16)
1 teaspoon baking powder
3 to 4 cloves garlic, crushed

Blend together eggs, water, salt, onion powder, and butter. Combine CGF flour with baking powder and whisk into wet ingredients until smooth. Stir in crushed garlic. Spoon batter onto hot waffle maker and cook for about 6 minutes or until waffles are a light golden tan.

Yield: about 6 waffles
Per serving: 10g fat, 18.3g total carbohydrate (2.3g fiber, 16g net carb), 3.8g protein, 179 calories.

Onion Waffles

¼ cup (56 g) butter
1 cup (160 g) finely chopped onion
2 eggs
1 cup (240 ml) water
¼ teaspoon salt
¼ teaspoon sage
¼ teaspoon thyme
¼ teaspoon black pepper
2 teaspoons onion powder
1 cup (136 g) CGF Flour Mix (page 16)
1 teaspoon baking powder

Waffles can be served with a variety of savory toppings such as eggs, ham, gravy, beef stew, or chopped meat.

Heat butter in a small sauté pan and cook onions until soft. Remove from heat and set aside to cool. In a bowl, blend together eggs, water, salt, sage, thyme, black pepper and onion powder. Combine CGF flour with baking powder and whisk into wet ingredients until smooth. Stir in cooked onions. Spoon batter onto hot waffle maker and cook for about 6 minutes or until waffles are a light golden brown. Serve at breakfast topped with a fried egg or sausage gravy, or serve for lunch or dinner topped with meat sauce or gravy or simply eat as a tasty slice of gluten-free bread.

Yield: about 6 waffles
Per serving: 10.1g fat, 20.7g total carbohydrate (2.8g fiber, 17.9g net carb), 4g protein, 188 calories.

Cheese Waffles
These waffles taste fantastic right out of the waffle iron. Leftover cheese waffles can be used as sandwich bread or cut into bite size pieces, dried, and served as croutons.

2 eggs
½ cup (120 ml) water
¼ teaspoon salt
1 teaspoon onion powder
¼ cup (56 g) butter, melted
½ cup (68 g) CGF Flour Mix (page 16)
1 teaspoon baking powder
1 cup (115 g) shredded sharp cheddar cheese

Blend together eggs, water, salt, onion powder, and butter. Combine CGF flour with baking powder and whisk into wet ingredients until smooth. Stir in cheese. Spoon batter onto hot waffle maker and cook for about 6 minutes or until waffles are a light golden brown.

Yield: about 4 waffles
Per serving: 123.8g fat, 14g total carbohydrate (1.7g fiber, 12.3g net carb), 11.4g protein, 315 calories.

Ham and Cheese Waffles
These waffles are sandwiches in themselves.

2 eggs
1 cup (240 ml) water
¼ teaspoon salt
¼ cup (56 g) butter, melted
1 cup (136 g) CGF Flour Mix (page 16)
1 teaspoon baking powder
1 cup (150 g) diced ham
1 cup (115 g) shredded sharp cheddar cheese

Blend together eggs, water, salt, and butter. Combine CGF flour with baking powder and whisk into wet ingredients until smooth. Stir in ham and cheese. Spoon batter onto hot waffle maker and cook for about 6 minutes or until waffles are a light golden brown.

Yield: about 6 waffles
Per serving: 18.5g fat, 18.7g total carbohydrate (2.3g fiber, 16.4g net carb), 12.5g protein, 293 calories.

Waffle Pizza
Waffles can make a crispy gluten-free crust for pizza.

2 eggs
½ cup (120 ml) water
¼ teaspoon salt
1 teaspoon onion powder
¼ teaspoon garlic powder
3 teaspoons (42 g) butter, melted
½ cup (68 g) CGF Flour Mix (page 16)
1 teaspoon baking powder
½ cup (55 g) shredded sharp cheddar cheese
Toppings for pizza, such as pizza sauce, cooked sausage, and mozzarella cheese.

Blend together eggs, water, salt, onion powder, garlic powder, and butter. Combine CGF flour with baking powder and whisk into wet ingredients until smooth. Stir in cheese. Spoon batter onto hot waffle maker and cook for about 6 minutes or until waffles are a light golden brown. Remove from waffle iron and let cool slightly. Cover waffles with pizza sauce, cooked sausage, and mozzarella cheese. Put on a cookie sheet and broil in the oven until the cheese is melted.

Yield: 4 serving size waffle pizzas
Per serving: 16g fat, 13.8g total carbohydrate (1.7g fiber, 12.1g net carb), 7.6g protein, 229 calories.

Gluten-Free French Toast
This chapter on gluten-free breakfast foods wouldn't be complete without including French toast. Here is our recipe using the bread recipes from Chapter 1.

1 egg
1 tablespoon (15 ml) milk
⅛ teaspoon vanilla extract
¼ teaspoon cinnamon

⅛ teaspoon nutmeg
Dash of salt
Coconut oil for frying
2 slices Leslie's Sandwich Bread (page 19)

In a wide-mouthed bowl, blend together egg, milk, vanilla extract, cinnamon, nutmeg, and salt. Heat coconut oil in skillet over medium heat. Dip the bread into the egg mixture, coating each side evenly. Place the bread onto a hot skillet. Cook until browned, then flip and cook the other side. Remove from heat and serve with topping of your choice.

Yield: 2 slices of toast
Per slice: 6.3g fat, 22.9g total carbohydrate (3.1g fiber, 19.8g net carb), 6.4g protein, 172 calories.

Peanut Butter and Banana Toast

This recipe uses Leslie's Sandwich Bread. It is basically a grilled peanut butter and banana sandwich.

1 tablespoon (16 g) peanut butter
2 slices Leslie's Sandwich Bread (page 19)
½ small banana, sliced
2 tablespoons (28 g) butter

Spread peanut butter on one side of a slice of bread. Place banana slices on top of the peanut butter, followed by the second slice of bread. Spread butter on the outside of one slice of bread and put it in a skillet, butter side down. While cooking, butter the top slice of bread. When the bottom slice of bread is toasted, flip and toast the remaining side. Remove from the pan, slice in half, and serve.

Yield: 1 sandwich
Per sandwich: 39.3g fat, 59.5g total carbohydrate (8.5g fiber, 51g net carb), 11.6g protein, 617 calories.

Jalapeno Pop-Ups

Jalapeno Pop-Ups swell as they cook, doubling in size, thus the reason for the name. Although they resemble muffins, they really aren't muffins. They aren't pancakes or waffles either, but they make a spectacular breakfast and that is why they are included it in this chapter.

4 eggs
½ cup (120 ml) coconut milk or whole milk
¼ teaspoon salt
5 tablespoons (30 g) CGF flour mix (page 16)
1 tablespoon (9 g) chopped jalapeno pepper
1 cup (120 g) shredded Monterey jack cheese

Preheat the oven to 425°F (220°C or gas mark 7).

With a blender or electric mixer, blend together eggs, milk, salt, and flour until there are no lumps and batter is slightly bubbly. Stir in jalapeno pepper. Pour batter into greased muffin cups. Sprinkle the cheese evenly over the batter in each muffin cup. Bake for 30 minutes. The batter will double in size while baking, but will shrink a little after they are removed from the oven and begin to cool. Eat like a muffin while they are still warm.

Yield: 6
Per serving: 9.7g fat, 6.8g total carbohydrate (0.7g fiber, 6.1g net carb), 9.8g protein, 154 calories.

4

Muffins

Making muffins using coconut flour is very simple. These recipes are so easy that even those who don't know anything about cooking can succeed. The recipes are not only simple, but tasty as well. When we serve these muffins to friends, they are totally surprised to hear that they are completely wheat-free and are even more amazed when we tell them that in place of wheat, we used finely ground coconut. With only a few exceptions, all of the muffin recipes in this chapter use coconut flour as the sole flour ingredient. In this chapter you will find a wide variety of muffins ranging from sweet muffins like maple nut, orange cranberry, gingerbread, carrot raisin, apple walnut, and orange mango, to savory such as jalapeno cheese (one of our favorites), chicken Asiago, garden vegetable, cheesy spinach, and even hot dog muffins.

All of the muffin recipes in this book are designed to make six muffins. If you want to make a dozen, simply double the recipe.

We highly recommend the use of our non-stick cooking oil for all these muffins because it prevents sticking and speeds cleanup better than any other oil. The recipe for our non-stick oil is on page 13. Make a cup or so of the oil and store it in your refrigerator so it will be there whenever you need it. It will last well over a year when stored in a cool place.

If you don't use our non-stick cooking oil, you will need to grease the muffin pans well with coconut oil or butter or use paper cupcake liners.

Maple Nut Muffins

3 eggs
2 tablespoons (28 g) butter, melted
¼ cup (60 ml) maple syrup
¼ teaspoon salt
½ teaspoon vanilla extract
¼ cup (32 g) coconut flour, sifted
¼ teaspoon baking powder
¼ cup (28 g) chopped pecans or walnuts

Preheat oven to 400°F (200°C or gas mark 6). Blend together eggs, butter, maple syrup, salt, and vanilla extract. Combine coconut flour with baking powder and whisk into batter until smooth. Stir in nuts. Pour batter into greased muffin cups. Bake in preheated oven for 18 minutes.

Yield: 6 muffins
Per serving: 10.1g fat, 12.9g total carbohydrate (2.3g fiber, 10.6g net carb), 4g protein, 155 calories.

Blueberry Almond Muffins.

Blueberry Almond Muffins

3 eggs
3 tablespoons (42 g) butter, melted
¼ cup (85 g) honey
¼ teaspoon salt
½ teaspoon almond extract
¼ cup (32 g) coconut flour, sifted
3 tablespoons (30 g) brown rice flour

¼ teaspoon baking powder
½ cup (75 g) fresh blueberries
¼ cup (28 g) sliced almonds

Preheat oven to 400°F (200°C or gas mark 6). Blend together eggs, butter, honey, salt, and almond extract. Combine coconut flour and brown rice flour with baking powder and whisk into batter until smooth. Stir in blueberries. Pour batter into greased muffin cups. Sprinkle almonds on top of the batter. Bake in preheated oven for 18 minutes.

Yield: 6 muffins
Per serving: 11.1g fat, 21.5g total carbohydrate (3g fiber, 18.5g net carb), 5.1g protein, 200 calories.

Blueberry Streusel Muffins

Streusel
½ cup (30 g) walnuts or pecans, chopped
2 tablespoons (30 g) brown sugar or coconut sugar
¼ teaspoon cinnamon
1 tablespoon (14 g) butter, softened

Mix together nuts, sugar, cinnamon, and butter and set aside.

Batter
3 eggs
2 tablespoons (28 g) butter, melted
⅓ cup (69 g) sugar
¼ teaspoon salt
¼ teaspoon vanilla extract
¼ cup (32 g) coconut flour, sifted
3 tablespoons (30 g) brown rice flour
¼ teaspoon baking powder
½ cup (75 g) fresh blueberries

Preheat oven to 400°F (200°C or gas mark 6). Blend together eggs, butter, sugar, salt, and vanilla extract. Combine coconut flour and brown

Blueberry Streusel Muffins.

rice flour with baking powder and whisk into batter until smooth. Stir in blueberries. Pour batter into greased muffin cups. Sprinkle streusel on top of the batter. Bake in preheated oven for 18 minutes.

Yield: 6 muffins
Per serving: 11.8g fat, 25.7g total carbohydrate (2.7g fiber, 23g net carb), 5.2g protein, 224 calories.

Orange Cranberry Muffins
These fruity muffins are ideal for breakfast. The secret behind these muffins is the orange juice concentrate, the product sold in the freezer section of the grocery store for making orange juice. It's almost like having a glass of orange juice in a muffin.

3 eggs
2 tablespoons (28 g) butter, melted

2 tablespoons (30 ml) orange juice concentrate, no water added
3 tablespoons (60 g) honey
¼ teaspoon salt
¼ teaspoon vanilla extract
¼ cup plus 1 teaspoon (35 g) coconut flour, sifted
¼ teaspoon baking powder
¼ cup (30 g) dried cranberries

Preheat oven to 400°F (200°C, or gas mark 6). Blend together eggs, butter, orange juice concentrate, honey, salt, and vanilla extract. Combine coconut flour with baking powder and whisk into batter until  smooth. Stir in cranberries. Pour batter into greased muffin cups. Bake in preheated oven for 15 to 16 minutes.

Yield: 6 muffins
Per serving: 3g fat, 12.8g total carbohydrate (2.3g fiber, 10.5g net carb), 3.7g protein, 91 calories.

Strawberry Cream Cheese Muffins
Who needs a bagel and cream cheese when you have these tasty muffins?

½ cup (115 g) cream cheese, softened
½ cup (90 g) chopped strawberries
3 eggs
¼ teaspoon salt
¼ teaspoon vanilla extract
½ cup (100 g) sugar
¼ cup plus 2 tablespoons (48 g) coconut flour, sifted
½ teaspoon baking powder

Preheat oven to 400°F (200°C or gas mark 6). Blend together cream cheese and strawberries and set aside. Whisk together eggs, salt, vanilla extract, and sugar. Blend cream cheese mixture into egg mixture. Combine coconut flour with baking powder and whisk into wet mixture until batter is smooth. Pour batter into greased muffin cups. Bake in preheated oven for 18-19 minutes.

Yield: 6 muffins
Per serving: 10g fat, 21.9g total carbohydrate (2.8g fiber, 19.1g net carb), 5.3g protein, 197 calories.

Gingerbread Muffins

3 eggs
2 tablespoons (28 g) butter, melted
¼ cup (60 g) packed brown sugar or coconut sugar
2 tablespoons (28 g) granulated sugar or Sucanat
1 tablespoon (20 g) molasses
1 teaspoon cinnamon
½ teaspoon ginger
⅛ teaspoon cloves
¼ teaspoon salt
¼ teaspoon vanilla extract
¼ cup (32 g) coconut flour, sifted
¼ teaspoon baking powder

Preheat oven to 400°F (200°C or gas mark 6). In a bowl, blend together first 10 ingredients. Add coconut flour and baking powder and whisk together until batter is smooth. Pour batter into greased muffin cups. Bake in preheated oven for 15 minutes.

Yield: 6 muffins
Per serving: 6.8g fat, 20.4g total carbohydrate (2.1g fiber, 18.3g net carb), 3.6g protein, 155 calories.

Zucchini Muffins

3 eggs
2 tablespoons (28 g) butter, melted
¼ cup (60 g) packed brown sugar or coconut sugar
2 tablespoons (28 g) granulated sugar or Sucanat
1 teaspoon cinnamon
⅛ teaspoon nutmeg
¼ teaspoon salt
¼ teaspoon vanilla extract
¼ cup (32 g) coconut flour, sifted
¼ teaspoon baking powder
½ cup (60 g) shredded zucchini
¼ cup (30 g) chopped walnuts

Preheat oven to 400°F (200°C or gas mark 6). In a bowl, blend together first eight ingredients. Combine coconut flour and baking powder and whisk together until batter is smooth. Stir in zucchini and nuts. Pour batter into greased muffin cups. Bake in preheated oven for 20 minutes.

Yield: 6 muffins
Per serving: 9.8g fat, 18.8g total carbohydrate (2.5g fiber, 16.3g net carb), 4.9g protein, 177 calories.

Cinnamon Apple Muffins

3 eggs
2 tablespoons (28 g) butter, melted
½ cup (100 g) coconut sugar or Sucanat
¼ teaspoon salt
½ teaspoon cinnamon
⅛ teaspoon nutmeg
¼ teaspoon almond extract
¼ cup (32 g) coconut flour, sifted
¼ teaspoon baking powder
½ cup (75 g) finely chopped tart apple

⅓ cup (50 g) raisins
¼ cup (30 g) chopped walnuts

Preheat oven to 400°F (200°C or gas mark 6). Blend together eggs, butter, sugar, salt, cinnamon, nutmeg, and almond extract. Combine coconut flour with baking powder and whisk into batter until smooth. Stir in apple, raisins, and walnuts. Pour batter into greased muffin cups. Bake in preheated oven for 20 minutes.

Yield: 6 muffins
Per serving: 9.8g fat, 28.8g total carbohydrate (2.9g fiber, 25.9g net carb), 5.1g protein, 215 calories.

Banana Peanut Muffins
Banana and peanuts in a muffin? Yes, these muffins are surprisingly delicious.

3 eggs
2 tablespoons (28 g) butter, melted
¼ cup (50 g) coconut sugar or Sucanat
¼ teaspoon salt
½ teaspoon vanilla extract
¼ cup (32 g) coconut flour, sifted
¼ teaspoon baking powder
½ medium banana, sliced and quartered
¼ cup (35 g) peanuts, halves and wholes
⅓ cup (58 g) sweet chocolate chips

Preheat oven to 400°F (200°C or gas mark 6). Blend together eggs, butter, sugar, salt, and vanilla extract. Combine coconut flour with baking powder and whisk into batter until smooth. Stir in banana, peanuts, and chocolate chips. Pour batter into greased muffin cups. Bake in preheated oven for 18 minutes.

Yield: 6 muffins
Per serving: 8.4g fat, 21.1g total carbohydrate (2.6g fiber, 18.5g net carb), 5.8g protein, 179 calories.

Date Nut Muffins

3 eggs
2 tablespoons (28 g) butter, melted
3 tablespoons (60 g) honey
¼ teaspoon salt
½ teaspoon vanilla extract
¼ cup (32 g) coconut flour, sifted
¼ teaspoon baking powder
¼ cup (28 g) chopped pecans or walnuts
½ cup (89 g) chopped dates

Preheat oven to 400°F (200°C or gas mark 6). Blend together eggs, butter, honey, salt, and vanilla extract. Combine coconut flour with baking powder and whisk into batter until smooth. Stir in nuts and dates. Pour batter into greased muffin cups. Bake in preheated oven for 18 minutes.

Yield: 6 muffins
Per serving: 10.2g fat, 23.2g total carbohydrate (3.5g fiber, 19.7g net carb), 4.4g protein, 192 calories.

Carrot Raisin Muffins

3 eggs
2 tablespoons (28 g) butter, melted
3 tablespoons (60 g) honey
¼ teaspoon salt
½ teaspoon allspice
¼ teaspoon cinnamon
1 tablespoon (15 ml) orange juice concentrate, no water added
¼ teaspoon vanilla extract
¼ cup (32 g) coconut flour, sifted
¼ teaspoon baking powder
½ cup (55 g) shredded carrot
½ cup (75 g) raisins

Preheat oven to 400°F (200°C or gas mark 6). Blend together eggs, butter, honey, salt, allspice, cinnamon, orange juice concentrate, and vanilla extract. Combine coconut flour with baking powder and whisk into batter until smooth. Stir in carrots and raisins. Pour batter into greased muffin cups. Bake in preheated oven for 22 to 23 minutes.

Yield: 6 muffins
Per serving: 6.9g fat, 22.5g total carbohydrate (2.6g fiber, 19.9g net carb), 4.1g protein, 161 calories.

Apple Walnut Muffins

3 eggs
2 tablespoons (28 g) butter, melted
1 tablespoon (15 ml) milk or coconut milk
½ cup (100 g) coconut sugar or Sucanat
¼ teaspoon salt
¼ teaspoon almond extract
¼ cup (32 g) coconut flour, sifted
¼ teaspoon baking powder
½ cup (60 g) chopped dried apple
¼ cup (30 g) chopped walnuts

Preheat oven to 400°F (200°C or gas mark 6). Blend together eggs, butter, milk, sugar, salt, and almond extract. Combine coconut flour with baking powder and whisk into batter until smooth. Stir in apple pieces and walnuts. Pour batter into greased muffin cups. Bake in preheated oven for 15 minutes.

Yield: 6 muffins
Per serving: 9.8g fat, 21.8g total carbohydrate (2.5g fiber, 19.3g net carb), 4.9g protein, 190 calories.

Apricot Muffins

3 eggs
2 tablespoons (28 g) butter, melted
1 tablespoon (15 ml) orange juice concentrate, no water added
½ cup (100 g) coconut sugar or Sucanat
¼ teaspoon salt
½ teaspoon vanilla extract
¼ cup (32 g) coconut flour, sifted
¼ teaspoon baking powder
½ cup (80 g) chopped dried apricots

Preheat oven to 400°F (200°C or gas mark 6). Blend together eggs, butter, orange juice concentrate, sugar, salt, and vanilla extract. Combine coconut flour with baking powder and whisk into batter until smooth. Stir in dried apricot. Pour batter into greased muffin cups. Bake in preheated oven for 18 minutes.

Yield: 6 muffins
Per serving: 6.8g fat, 21.6g total carbohydrate (2.2g fiber, 19.4g net carb), 3.8g protein, 160 calories.

Cherry Muffins
The dried cherries in these muffins absorb moisture while they are cooking. The end product tastes remarkably similar to cherry pie. One of the ingredients in this recipe is apple cherry juice concentrate. This is available at most grocery stores in the frozen juices section. If you prefer, you can substitute orange juice concentrate.

3 eggs
2 tablespoons (28 g) butter, melted
2 tablespoons (15 ml) apple cherry juice concentrate, no water added
⅓ cup (69 g) sugar
¼ teaspoon salt
¼ teaspoon almond extract
¼ cup plus 1 teaspoon (35 g) coconut flour, sifted

¼ teaspoon baking powder
½ cup (60 g) chopped dried tart cherries

Preheat oven to 400°F (200°C or gas mark 6). Blend together eggs, butter, apple cherry juice concentrate, sugar, salt, and almond extract. Combine coconut flour with baking powder and whisk into batter until smooth. Stir in cherries. Pour batter into greased muffin cups. Bake in preheated oven for 18 minutes.

Yield: 6 muffins
Per serving: 6.8g fat, 19.5g total carbohydrate (2g fiber, 17.5g net carb), 3.6g protein, 152 calories.

Orange Mango Muffins

This recipe calls for orange peach mango juice concentrate. This is available at most grocery stores in the frozen juices section. If you can't find it in your store, you can substitute orange juice concentrate.

3 eggs
2 tablespoons (28 g) butter, melted
2 tablespoons (15 ml) orange peach mango juice concentrate,
   no water added
⅓ cup (69 g) sugar
¼ teaspoon salt
¼ teaspoon vanilla extract
¼ cup plus 1 teaspoon (35 g) coconut flour, sifted
¼ teaspoon baking powder
½ cup (60 g) finely chopped dried mangos

Preheat oven to 400°F (200°C or gas mark 6). Blend together eggs, butter, orange peach mango juice concentrate, sugar, salt, and vanilla extract. Combine coconut flour with baking powder and whisk into batter until smooth. Stir in dried mangos. Pour batter into greased muffin cups. Bake in preheated oven for 18 to 20 minutes.

Yield: 6 muffins
Per serving: 6.8g fat, 16.6g total carbohydrate (2.1g fiber, 14.5g net carb), 3.6g protein, 140 calories.

Very Berry Muffins

These muffins are like little individual servings of berry cobbler. You can use any combination of blueberries, raspberries, boysenberries, and blackberries, or use just a single type of berry. It's your choice. Make sure berries are dry, not wet, as the additional moisture will affect the end product. Cut large berries in half so they are all about equal in volume.

3 eggs
2 tablespoons (28 g) butter, melted
⅓ cup (69 g) sugar
¼ teaspoon salt
2 tablespoons (30 ml) orange juice concentrate, no water added
¼ cup (32 g) coconut flour, sifted
2 tablespoons (20 g) brown rice flour
¼ teaspoon baking powder
¾ cup (110 g) fresh berries (blueberries, raspberries, boysenberries, or blackberries)

Preheat oven to 400°F (200°C or gas mark 6). Blend together eggs, butter, sugar, salt, and orange juice concentrate. Combine coconut flour and brown rice flour with baking powder and whisk into batter until smooth. Pour batter into greased muffin cups. Spoon an equal amount of berries onto the top and center of each muffin and push them down *slightly* into the batter. Bake in preheated oven for 18 minutes. When cooked, the berries will form a slight depression in the center of each muffin.

Yield: 6 muffins
Per serving: 7g fat, 20g total carbohydrate (3.2g fiber, 16.8g net carb), 4.1g protein, 156 calories.

Apple Kiwi Muffins

The name of these muffins comes from the apple kiwi strawberry juice concentrate used in the recipe. Apple juice is the primary ingredient in this juice, so we've added fresh chopped kiwis to boost the kiwi flavor If you can't find apple kiwi strawberry juice concentrate you can substitute it with apple juice concentrate.

3 eggs
2 tablespoons (28 g) butter, melted
2 tablespoons (30 ml) apple kiwi strawberry juice concentrate, no water added
⅓ cup (69 g) sugar
¼ teaspoon salt
½ teaspoon vanilla extract
¼ cup plus 1 tablespoon (40 g) coconut flour, sifted
¼ teaspoon baking powder
1 kiwi, finely chopped

Preheat oven to 400°F (200°C or gas mark 6). Blend together eggs, butter, concentrate, sugar, salt, and vanilla extract. Combine coconut flour with baking powder and whisk into batter until smooth. Fold in kiwi. Pour batter into greased muffin cups. Bake in preheated oven for 20 minutes.

Yield: 6 muffins
Per serving: 7.1g fat, 19.3g total carbohydrate (2.8g fiber, 16.5g net carb), 3.9g protein, 154 calories.

Cheese Puffins

These cheese mushroom muffins are so light and airy they are more of a cross between a cheese puff and a muffin, thus the name "puffins."

3 eggs, separated
3 tablespoons (28 g) butter, melted
¼ teaspoon salt
½ teaspoon onion powder
3 tablespoons (24 g) coconut flour, sifted
¼ teaspoon baking powder
¾ cup (55 g) chopped mushrooms
½ cup (58 g) shredded Gouda cheese or other hard cheese
¾ cup (90 g) shredded sharp cheddar cheese

Preheat oven to 400°F (200°C or gas mark 6). Beat egg whites until stiff peaks form, then set aside.

Blend together egg yolks, butter, salt, and onion powder. Combine coconut flour with baking powder and whisk into batter until smooth. Stir in mushrooms and Gouda cheese. Fold in half of the egg whites just enough to mix into the batter but do not over mix. Pour batter into greased muffin cups. Fold cheddar cheese into the remaining egg whites and spoon an even portion onto the top of each muffin cup. Bake for 18 minutes or until muffins are golden brown.

Yield: 6 muffins
Per serving: 16.2g fat, 3.3g total carbohydrate (1.5g fiber, 1.8g net carb), 9.8g protein, 197 calories.

Jalapeno Cheese Muffins

These are one of our favorite gluten-free muffins. The amount of jalapeno peppers used in this recipe is just enough for those who don't especially like spicy hot foods. If you relish the heat, add another 1 to 2 tablespoons of jalapenos.

3 eggs
3 tablespoons (28 g) butter, melted
¼ teaspoon salt
½ teaspoon onion powder
1 tablespoon (15 ml) milk or coconut milk
¼ cup (32 g) coconut flour, sifted
¼ teaspoon baking powder
2 tablespoons (30 g) chopped jalapeno peppers
¾ cup (90 g) shredded sharp cheddar cheese, divided in half

Preheat oven to 400°F (200°C or gas mark 6). Blend together eggs, butter, salt, onion powder, and milk. Combine coconut flour with baking powder and whisk into batter until smooth. Stir in jalapeno peppers and half of the shredded cheese. Pour batter into greased muffin cups. Top eat muffin with the remaining cheese. Bake in preheated oven for 15 minutes.

Yield: 6 muffins
Per serving: 13.8g fat, 3.9g total carbohydrate (2g fiber, 1.9g net carb), 7.5g protein, 169 calories.

Chicken Asiago Muffins

These muffins are named for the chicken and Asiago cheese used in the recipe. Asiago is a hard Italian cheese. It has a sharp but pleasant flavor that mellows when cooked.

3 tablespoons (42 g) butter, melted
¼ cup (40 g) chopped onion
¾ cup (57 g) chopped mushrooms
3 eggs
¼ teaspoon salt
¼ teaspoon black pepper
½ teaspoon onion powder
⅛ teaspoons celery seed
1 tablespoon (15 ml) milk or coconut milk
¼ cup (32 g) coconut flour, sifted
¼ teaspoon baking powder
¾ cup (90 g) shredded Asiago cheese
1 cup (140 g) finely chopped chicken

Preheat oven to 400°F (200°C or gas mark 6). In a skillet with 1 tablespoon (14 g) of butter, lightly sauté onions and mushrooms until onions are crisp tender, about two minutes. Remove from heat and set aside to cool.

In a bowl, blend together eggs, 2 tablespoons (28 g) butter, salt, black pepper, onion powder, celery seed, and milk. Combine coconut flour and baking powder and whisk into batter until smooth. Stir in cooked vegetables, cheese, and chicken. Pour batter into greased muffin cups. Bake in preheated oven for 18 to 20 minutes.

Yield: 6 muffins
Per serving: 13.8g fat, 3.8g total carbohydrate (2g fiber, 1.8g net carb), 14.5g protein, 198 calories.

Garden Vegetable Muffins

These muffins are loaded with vegetables and accented with Asiago cheese.

¼ cup (40 g) chopped onion
¾ cup (57 g) chopped mushrooms
¼ cup (14 g) finely chopped sundried tomatoes
3 eggs
2 tablespoons (28 g) butter, melted
½ teaspoon salt
¼ teaspoon black pepper
½ teaspoon marjoram
¼ cup (32 g) coconut flour, sifted
¼ teaspoon baking powder
¾ cup (90 g) shredded zucchini
¾ cup (90 g) shredded Asiago cheese

Preheat oven to 400°F (200°C or gas mark 6). In a skillet with a little butter or coconut oil, lightly sauté onions, mushrooms, and sundried tomatoes until onions are crisp tender, about two minutes. Remove from heat and set aside to cool.

In a bowl, blend together eggs, butter, salt, black pepper, and marjoram. Combine coconut flour and baking powder and whisk into batter until smooth. Stir in cooked vegetables, zucchini, and cheese. Pour batter into greased muffin cups. Bake in preheated oven for 20 minutes.

Yield: 6 muffins
Per serving: 11.2g fat, 5.9g total carbohydrate (2.5g fiber, 3.4g net carb), 8.2g protein, 155 calories.

Bacon Omelet Muffins

½ cup (80 g) chopped onion
¾ cup (57 g) chopped mushrooms
3 eggs
2 tablespoons (28 g) butter, melted
½ teaspoon salt
¼ teaspoon black pepper
¼ cup (32 g) coconut flour, sifted
¼ teaspoon baking powder
6 strips bacon, cooked crisp and crumbled

Preheat oven to 400°F (200°C or gas mark 6). In a skillet with a little butter or bacon drippings, lightly sauté onions and mushrooms until onions are crisp tender. Remove from heat and set aside to cool.

In a bowl, blend together eggs, butter, salt, and black pepper. Combine coconut flour and baking powder and whisk into batter until smooth. Stir in cooked vegetables and bacon. Pour batter into greased muffin cups. Bake in preheated oven for 17 to 18 minutes.

Yield: 6 muffins
Per serving: 14.8g fat, 5g total carbohydrate (2.2g fiber, 2.8g net carb), 11g protein, 198 calories.

Variation: If you like cheese on your omelet, you can add shredded sharp cheddar cheese on top of each muffin just before baking.

Louisiana Shrimp Muffins
This recipe is almost like eating jambalaya in a muffin.

3 tablespoons (42 g) butter, melted
¼ cup (40 g) chopped onion
2 tablespoons (20 g) finely chopped red bell pepper
⅓ cup (18 g) finely chopped sundried tomatoes
1 cup (115 g) cooked baby shrimp
3 eggs
½ teaspoon salt
½ teaspoon onion powder
2 teaspoons Cajun seasoning
¼ cup (32 g) coconut flour, sifted
¼ teaspoon baking powder

Preheat oven to 400°F (200°C or gas mark 6). Heat 1 tablespoon (14 g) of butter in a skillet and lightly sauté onions and bell peppers for 1 to 2 minutes. Add sundried tomatoes and shrimp and continue cooking for another minute or until vegetables are crisp tender. Remove from heat and set aside.

Blend together eggs, 2 tablespoons (28 g) butter, salt, onion powder, and Cajun seasoning. Combine coconut flour with baking powder and whisk into batter until smooth. Stir in vegetable mixture. Pour batter into greased muffin cups. Bake in preheated oven for 22 minutes.

Yield: 6 muffins
Per serving: 9g fat, 5.2g total carbohydrate (2.3g fiber, 2.9g net carb), 8.1g protein, 133 calories.

Corn Muffins

3 tablespoons (42 g) butter, melted
½ cup (80 g) chopped onion
2 tablespoons (20 g) finely chopped red bell pepper
⅓ cup (45 g) whole kernel corn
4 eggs
½ teaspoon salt
¼ teaspoon black pepper
½ teaspoon onion powder
¼ cup (32 g) coconut flour, sifted
1 tablespoon (9 g) corn meal
¼ teaspoon baking powder

Preheat oven to 400°F (200°C, or gas mark 6). Heat butter in a skillet and lightly sauté onions and bell peppers for 1 to 2 minutes. Add corn and continue cooking for another minute or until vegetables are crisp tender. Remove from heat and set aside.

Blend together eggs, salt, black pepper, and onion powder. Combine coconut flour and corn meal with baking powder and whisk into batter until smooth. Stir in vegetable mixture. Pour batter into greased muffin cups.

Bake in preheated oven for 18 minutes.

Yield: 6 muffins
Per serving: 3.8g fat, 6g total carbohydrate (4.8g fiber, 1.2g net carb), 4.8g protein, 77 calories.

Variation: Add some kick to these muffins by stirring in 1 to 2 tablespoons of finely chopped Jalapeno peppers into the batter just before baking.

Ham and Egg Muffins

This is a gluten-free version of McDonald's Egg McMuffin. Our version is more like a traditional muffin that is stuffed with ham and eggs instead of a sandwich made with an English muffin. You will cook an egg yolk in each muffin cup. When you separate the yolks from the whites, make sure not to break the yolks!

4 ounces (110 g) thinly sliced ham
6 eggs, separated
¼ cup (56 g) butter, melted
½ teaspoon salt
⅛ teaspoon black pepper
¼ cup (32 g) coconut flour, sifted
¼ teaspoon baking powder
2 tablespoons (30 ml) milk or coconut milk
¾ cup (90 g) shredded sharp cheddar cheese, divided in half

Preheat oven to 400°F (200°C or gas mark 6). Cut ham to fit inside muffin cups. Grease muffin cups and place ham on the bottom of each cup. Blend together egg whites, butter, salt, and black pepper. Combine coconut flour with baking powder and whisk into batter until smooth. Stir in half of the shredded cheese. Pour half of the batter into the muffin cups on top of the ham. Make an indentation in the center of the batter of each cup with a spoon and place one unbroken egg yolk in each one. Mix 2 tablespoons (30 ml) of milk into the remaining batter and pour the batter over the egg yolks. If the batter is too thick, thin it slightly

The Ham and Egg Muffin is characterized by the egg yolk in center of each muffin.

with a little milk or melted butter. Top the batter with the remaining shredded cheese. Bake for 18 to 20 minutes.

Yield: 6 muffins
Per serving: 17.8g fat, 3.8g total carbohydrate (1.9g fiber, 1.9g net carb), 10.3g protein, 215 calories.

Cheesy Spinach Muffins

This vegetable cheese muffin can be made with spinach or any other leafy green, such as chard or kale.

3 eggs
2 tablespoons (28 g) butter, melted
¼ teaspoon salt
¼ cup (32 g) coconut flour, sifted
¼ teaspoon baking powder

½ cup (80 g) chopped onion
¾ cup (57 g) chopped mushrooms
¾ cup (90 g) shredded sharp cheddar cheese
1 cup (60 g) chopped spinach or kale

Preheat oven to 400°F (200°C or gas mark 6). In a bowl, blend together eggs, butter, and salt. Combine coconut flour and baking powder and whisk into batter until smooth. Stir in onion, mushrooms, and ½ cup (30 g) of cheese. Mix half of the spinach into the batter. Layer the other half evenly into the bottom of each greased muffin cup. Pour batter into the muffin cups. Top each muffin with the remaining ¼ cup (15 g) of cheese. Bake in preheated oven for 16 minutes.

Yield: 6 muffins
Per serving: 11.8g fat, 5.3g total carbohydrate (2.4g fiber, 2.9g net carb), 8g protein, 158 calories.

Hot Dog Muffins
Here is a treat the kids and even parents will enjoy. These muffins taste much like the traditional hot dog on a bun, but without the gluten.

3 hot dogs
3 eggs
2 tablespoons (28 g) coconut oil, melted
¼ teaspoon salt
½ teaspoon prepared mustard
¼ cup (32 g) coconut flour, sifted
¼ teaspoon baking powder
¼ cup (40 g) diced onions
3 tablespoons (45 g) pickle relish, drained
½ cup (58 g) shredded sharp cheddar cheese

Preheat oven to 400°F (200°C or gas mark 6). Slice each hot dog into about 20 to 22 pieces and set aside.

In a bowl, blend together eggs, coconut oil, salt, and mustard. Combine coconut flour and baking powder and whisk into wet mixture until batter is smooth. Stir in cut meat, onions, and pickle relish. Make sure to drain all the water from the pickle relish. Pour batter into greased muffin cups. Top each muffin with an equal portion of shredded cheese. Bake for 16 to 18 minutes.

Yield: 6 muffins
Per serving: 12.6g fat, 7.5g total carbohydrate (2.1g fiber, 5.4g net carb), 8.5g protein, 178 calories.

Bratwurst and Sauerkraut Muffins

When you first see the name of these muffins you might be surprised, since bratwurst and sauerkraut are not foods ordinarily associated with muffins. However, these muffins taste quite good, much like eating a traditional bratwurst sandwich with all the trimmings.

1 bratwurst
2 tablespoons (28 g) coconut oil
3 eggs
¼ teaspoon salt
¼ teaspoon dill
½ teaspoon prepared mustard
¼ cup (32 g) coconut flour, sifted
¼ teaspoon baking powder
¼ cup (40 g) diced onions
½ cup (60 g) sauerkraut, drained
3 tablespoons (45 g) pickle relish, drained

Preheat oven to 400°F (200°C or gas mark 6). Fry bratwurst in coconut oil until lightly browned. Remove from heat and let cool. Cut the bratwurst into about 18 slices, then cut each slice in half. Combine with the oil in the pan and set aside.

In a bowl, blend together eggs, salt, dill, and mustard. Combine coconut flour and baking powder and whisk into wet mixture until batter is smooth. Stir in cut bratwurst, coconut oil, onions, sauerkraut, and pickle relish. Make sure to drain all the water from the sauerkraut and pickle relish. Pour the batter into greased muffin cups. Bake for 18-20 minutes.

Yield: 6 muffins
Per serving: 11.7g fat, 7.4g total carbohydrate (2.4g fiber, 5g net carb), 5.7g protein, 156 calories.

Pulled Pork Muffins

This muffin uses pulled or shredded pork. It tastes similar to a barbeque pork sandwich. If you prefer, you can substitute beef or chicken for the pork.

3 eggs
2 tablespoons (28 g) coconut oil, melted
1 tablespoon (15 ml) milk or coconut milk
¼ teaspoon salt
¼ teaspoon garlic powder
¼ teaspoon onion powder
¼ cup (32 g) coconut flour, sifted
¼ teaspoon baking powder
1 cup (200 g) pulled or shredded pork
¼ cup (40 g) finely chopped onion
2 tablespoons (32 g) barbeque sauce
½ cup (58 g) shredded sharp cheddar cheese

Preheat oven to 400°F (200°C or gas mark 6). In a bowl, blend together eggs, coconut oil, milk, salt, garlic powder, and onion powder. Combine coconut flour and baking powder and whisk into wet mixture until batter is smooth. Stir in meat and onions. Pour the batter into greased muffin cups. Spoon 1 teaspoon of barbeque sauce on top of each muffin. Top each muffin with an equal portion of cheese. Bake for 15 to 16 minutes.

Yield: 6 muffins
Per serving: 15.3g fat, 6g total carbohydrate (2g fiber, 4g net carb), 14.5g protein, 221 calories.

5

Cakes

Coconut flour makes delicious cakes. The flour, with eggs as a binder and leavening agent, is very well suited for cake making. Many cakes, like our Carrot Raisin Cake, can be made using coconut flour without any additional flours. However, the addition of a little brown rice flour in some recipes improves the taste and texture. These recipes include Vanilla Cake, Ganache-Covered Strawberry Layer Cake, Bavarian Layer Cake, and the Black Forest Cake. In addition to traditional cakes, you will find several cupcake recipes, fruit and nut tarts, and other novelty cakes such as Lamingtons—a popular Australian snack and dessert cake.

We recommend that you use our non-stick cooking oil for greasing all of your baking pans. The recipe for this oil is found on page 13. This oil works better than most other oils for preventing sticking. Cakes come out of the pans with less effort and cookware cleans up quickly. You can make as much or as little as you want. A cup's worth can last months. When stored it in the refrigerator it can last well over a year. We have had some that is four years old and works and tastes just as good as the day it was made.

If you don't use our non-stick cooking oil, you will need to coat the pans with another oil and dust them lightly with brown rice flour or use a cooking liner to prevent sticking. The liners work exceptionally well.

Vanilla Cake with Strawberry Whipped Cream Frosting

This cake tastes very similar to strawberry shortcake. The whipped cream frosting can be made using pureed fresh strawberries or strawberry jam.

Frosting
1 cup (240 ml) heavy cream
½ teaspoon vanilla extract
2 tablespoons (26 g) granulated sugar
⅓ cup (106 g) strawberry jam or puree

Combine cream and vanilla extract in a bowl. Whip until soft peaks form. Add strawberry jam and sugar and whip until stiff peaks form. For best results make sure the cream and jam are well chilled before using. If not using immediately, cover and keep refrigerated.

Cake

8 eggs
½ cup (112 g) butter, melted
1 cup (100 g) sugar
1 teaspoon salt
1 teaspoon vanilla extract
½ cup (80 g) brown rice flour
¾ cup (100 g) coconut flour, sifted
1 teaspoon baking powder

Preheat oven to 350°F (180°C or gas mark 4). Using an electric mixer, blend together eggs, butter, sugar, salt, and vanilla extract. Combine brown rice flour, coconut flour, and baking powder and blend into wet mixture until batter is smooth. Pour batter into a greased 11 x 7 x 2-inch (28 x 18 x 5-cm) baking dish. Bake for 30 to 35 minutes or until a toothpick inserted into the center of the cake comes out clean. Remove the cake from the oven and cool. Serve each slice with a generous scoop of strawberry whipped cream frosting. Sliced fresh strawberries can be added as a garnish.

Yield: 12 servings
Per serving: 13g fat, 29.5g total carbohydrate (3.2g fiber, 26.3g net carb), 5.6g protein, 256 calories.

Ganache-Covered Strawberry Layer Cake

This recipe consists of four layers of cake each separated by a strawberry cream filling and covered with ganache frosting. Ganache is a chocolate- and cream-based frosting that is very simple to make and delicious.

Ganache Frosting

1 cup (175 g) semi-sweet chocolate chips
½ cup (120 ml) heavy cream
Fresh strawberries for garnish

Place chocolate chips in a bowl. Heat heavy cream on medium-high heat until it comes to a boil. Remove from heat and immediately pour cream over chocolate chips. Let it sit for a few minutes to melt the chocolate chips. Using an electric mixer, blend until the mixture has a uniform color and creamy texture. Set aside to cool. The longer you allow the ganache to cool, the thicker it will become.

Filling

8 ounces (225 g) cream cheese, softened
¼ cup (55 g) butter, softened
¾ cup (240 g) strawberry jam

Blend cream cheese with butter using an electric mixer. Gradually add strawberry jam until mixture is fully blended and of uniform texture.

Cake

12 eggs
½ cup (110 g) butter
½ cup (120 ml) milk
1¼ cup (250 g) sugar
1 teaspoon salt
2 teaspoons vanilla extract
½ cup (80 g) brown rice flour
1 cup (128 g) coconut flour, sifted
1½ teaspoons baking powder

Preheat oven to 350°F (180°C or gas mark 4). Using an electric mixer, blend together eggs, butter, milk, sugar, salt, and vanilla extract. Stir in brown rice flour. Combine coconut flour and baking powder and blend into wet mixture until batter is smooth. Pour batter into two greased 9 x 9 x 2-inch (23 x 23 x 5-cm) round baking pans. Bake for 30 to 35 minutes or until a toothpick inserted in the center of the cake comes out clean. Remove cake from oven and cool for 5 to 10 minutes. Carefully remove the cake from the pans and cool to room temperature.

Slice each cake in half lengthwise, making four thin layers. Spread one-third of the strawberry filling over the top of the first layer of cake. Place a second layer of cake on top and cover the top with another one-third of the filling. Put the third layer on and cover the top with the remaining filling. Place the fourth layer of cake on top. Cover the entire cake, top and sides, evenly with the ganache frosting. Remove the stems from the strawberries. Slice each berry in half and place around the outer top edge of the cake. The cake can be eaten immediately or saved for later. However, if you allow the cake to rest for several hours or overnight the frosting will set, forming a semi-hard glaze.

Yield: 16 servings
Per serving: 21.6g fat, 40.9g total carbohydrate (3.4g fiber, 37.5g net carb), 7.9g protein, 387 calories.

Bavarian Layer Cake

This cake originated in Bavaria, Germany. In German, it is called Prinzregententorte. We simply call it Bavarian Layer Cake. Traditionally, it consists of six thin layers of sponge cake separated by chocolate buttercream filling and topped with a dark chocolate glaze frosting. This version is simplified to just four layers.

Frosting

1 cup (175 g) semi-sweet chocolate chips
½ cup (120 ml) heavy cream

Place chocolate chips in a bowl. Heat heavy cream on medium-high heat until it comes to a boil. Remove from heat and immediately pour cream over chocolate chips. Let it sit for a few minutes to melt the chocolate chips. Using an electric mixer, blend until the mixture has a uniform color and creamy texture. Set aside to cool. The longer you allow the frosting to cool, the thicker it will become.

Filling

1 cup (225 g) butter, softened
3 cups (360 g) powdered sugar
½ cup (40 g) cocoa powder
1 teaspoon almond extract
¼ cup (60 ml) heavy cream or whole milk

Cream butter, 2 cups of sugar, and cocoa powder using an electric mixer. Add remaining 1 cup of sugar, almond extract, and cream and blend together until smooth.

Cake

12 eggs
½ cup (110 g) butter
½ cup (120 ml) milk
1¼ cup (250 g) sugar
1 teaspoon salt
2 teaspoons vanilla extract
½ cup (80 g) brown rice flour
1 cup (128 g) coconut flour, sifted
1½ teaspoons baking powder

Preheat oven to 350°F (180°C or gas mark 4). Using an electric mixer, blend together eggs, butter, milk, sugar, salt, and vanilla extract. Stir in brown rice flour. Combine coconut flour and baking powder and blend into wet mixture until batter is smooth. Pour batter into two greased 9 x 9 x 2-inch (23 x 23 x 5-cm) round baking pans. Bake for 30 to 35 minutes or until a toothpick inserted in the center of the cake comes out clean. Remove cake from oven and cool for 5 to 10 minutes. Carefully remove the cake from the pans and cool to room temperature.

Slice each cake in half lengthwise, making four thin layers. Spread one-third of the chocolate buttercream filling over the top of the first layer of cake. Place a second layer of cake on the first and cover the top with another one-third of the filling. Put the third layer on the second and cover with the remaining filling. Place the fourth layer of cake on top. Cover the entire cake, top and sides, evenly with the frosting. The cake can be eaten immediately or saved for later. However, if you allow the cake to rest for several hours or overnight the frosting will set, forming a semi-hard glaze.

Yield: 16 servings
Per serving: 25.5g fat, 53.8g total carbohydrate (3.4g fiber, 50.4g net carb), 7g protein, 466 calories.

Carrot Raisin Cake

The only flour used in this cake is coconut flour. The cream cheese frosting makes this carrot cake incredibly delicious.

Frosting

6 ounces (169 g) cream cheese, softened
¼ cup (56 g) butter, softened
1 teaspoon vanilla extract
½ cup (60 g) powdered sugar
½ cup (60 g) chopped walnuts

Combine all of the frosting ingredients except for the walnuts into a bowl and with an electric mixer, blend together until smooth.

Cake

10 eggs
½ cup (112 g) butter, melted
½ cup (120 ml) orange juice concentrate, no water added
½ cup (38 g) unpacked brown sugar or coconut sugar
1 cup (100 g) sugar
1 teaspoon salt
½ teaspoon vanilla extract
1½ teaspoons cinnamon
1 teaspoon nutmeg
½ teaspoon cloves
1 cup (128 g) coconut flour, sifted
2 teaspoon baking powder
2 cups (220 g) shredded carrot
½ cup (73 g) raisins

Preheat oven to 350°F (180°C or gas mark 4). Using an electric mixer, blend together eggs, butter, orange juice concentrate, sugars, salt, vanilla extract, cinnamon, nutmeg, and cloves. Combine coconut flour and baking powder and blend into wet mixture until batter is smooth. Stir in carrot and raisins. Pour batter into greased 11 x 7 x 2-inch (28 x 18 x 5-cm) baking dish. Bake for 40 minutes or until a toothpick inserted in the center of the cake comes out clean. Remove cake from oven and cool. Cover with frosting and top with walnuts.

Yield: 16 servings
Per serving: 18.3g fat, 23.4g total carbohydrate (3.7g fiber, 19.7g net carb), 6.7g protein, 279 calories.

Black Forest Cake

This is our gluten-free version of the popular four layer chocolate cake covered in whipped cream frosting.

Frosting and Filling

1¾ cups (660 ml) heavy cream
1½ teaspoons vanilla extract
3 teaspoons or 1 packet unflavored gelatin
⅓ cup (69 g) granulated sugar
1 can (14.5 ounces/430 g) pitted tart cherries, for filling
Maraschino cherries for garnish
1 ounce (28 g) square semi-sweet baking chocolate, shaved for garnish

Whip the cream with an electric mixer until soft peaks form. Add one at a time the vanilla, gelatin, and sugar. Continue to whip until stiff peaks form. Do not over whip or the cream will turn into butter. For best results, make sure the cream is well chilled before using. If you are not frosting the cake immediately, cover the whipped cream and keep refrigerated. The gelatin is an important addition to this recipe because it stabilizes the whipped cream, giving it more body and keeps it from separating.

Cake

8 (1 ounce/28 g) squares semi-sweet baking chocolate
1¼ cups (446 g) butter
12 eggs
½ cup (120 ml) milk
1¾ cup (350 g) sugar
1 teaspoon salt
2 teaspoons vanilla extract

¼ cup (40 g) brown rice flour
1 cup (128 g) coconut flour, sifted
½ teaspoon baking powder

Preheat oven to 350°F (180°C or gas mark 4). Combine baking chocolate and ¾ cup (336 g) butter in a saucepan and cook over medium-low heat, stirring frequently, until chocolate is completely melted. Blend the chocolate and butter together until evenly mixed. Set aside to cool.

Using an electric mixer, blend together eggs, ½ cup (110g) butter (softened), milk, sugar, salt, and vanilla extract. Blend in chocolate mixture. Stir in brown rice flour. Combine coconut flour and baking powder and blend into wet mixture until batter is smooth. Pour batter into two greased 9 x 9 x 2-inch (23 x 23 x 5-cm) round baking pans. Bake for 30 to 35 minutes or until a toothpick inserted in the center of the cake comes out clean. Remove cake from the oven and cool for 5 to 10 minutes. Carefully remove the cake from the pans and cool to room temperature.

Slice each cake in half making four thin layers. Spread a layer of whipped cream frosting over the top of the first layer of cake followed by ⅓ of the pitted cherries. Place a second layer of cake on top and cover with another layer of frosting and ⅓ of the pitted cherries. Put the third layer on top and cover with another layer of frosting and the remaining pitted cherries. Place the fourth layer of cake on top. Cover the entire cake with the remaining whipped cream frosting. Garnish with maraschino cherries and chocolate shavings.

Yield: 16 servings
Per serving: 30.2g fat, 43.9g total carbohydrate (3.2g fiber, 40.7g net carb), 7g protein, 469 calories.

Lamingtons
Lamingtons are a popular Australian dessert made of sponge cake, dipped in chocolate frosting, and rolled in desiccated coconut.

Frosting
1½ cups (260 g) semi-sweet chocolate chips
2 tablespoon (26 g) sugar

½ cup (120 ml) heavy cream
Flaked or desiccated coconut

Place chocolate chips and sugar in a bowl. Heat heavy cream on medium-high heat until it comes to a boil. Remove from heat and immediately pour cream over chocolate chips. Let it sit for a few minutes to melt the chocolate chips. Using an electric mixer, blend until the mixture has a uniform color and creamy texture. Set aside to cool. The longer you allow the frosting to cool, the dryer it will become.

Cake
9 eggs
½ cup (110 g) butter
¼ cup (60 ml) milk
¾ cup (150 g) sugar
½ teaspoon salt
1 teaspoon vanilla extract
2 tablespoons (20 g) brown rice flour
¾ cup (96 g) coconut flour, sifted
½ teaspoon baking powder

Preheat oven to 350°F (180°C or gas mark 4). Using an electric mixer, blend together eggs, butter, milk, sugar, salt, and vanilla extract. Stir in brown rice flour. Combine coconut flour and baking powder and blend into wet mixture until batter is smooth. Pour batter into a greased 11 x 7 x 2-inch (28 x 18 x 5-cm) baking dish. Bake for 30 to 35 minutes or until a toothpick inserted in the center of the cake comes out clean. Remove the cake from the oven and cool for 5 to 10 minutes. Carefully remove the cake from the baking dish and cool on a wire rack to room temperature.

Slice the cake into 15 individual servings. Dip each slice into the chocolate frosting, coating both sides. Roll the cake in flaked coconut and set on wax paper or wire rack to dry. Frosting will thicken over time.

Yield: 15 servings
Per serving: 16.8g fat, 27.8g total carbohydrate (3.4g fiber, 24.4g net carb), 6.1g protein, 285 calories.

Lamingtons are little chocolate covered cakes rolled in desiccated coconut.

Vanilla Chocolate Chip Cupcakes

These easy-to-make cupcakes are so good they don't need any frosting. If you want to dress them up a bit, add a tablespoon (6 g) of unsweetened shredded coconut or sliced almonds to the top of each cupcake before baking.

3 eggs
3 tablespoons (42 g) butter, melted
⅓ cup (69 g) sugar
½ teaspoon vanilla extract
¼ teaspoon salt
¼ cup (32 g) coconut flour, sifted
¼ teaspoon baking powder
¼ cup (25 g) semi-sweet chocolate chips

Preheat oven to 400°F (200°C or gas mark 6). Stir together eggs, butter, sugar, vanilla extract, and salt. Combine coconut flour and baking powder and whisk into wet mixture until batter is smooth. Stir in chocolate chips. Bake for 15 minutes.

Yield: 6 cupcakes
Per serving: 9.9g fat, 17.1g total carbohydrate (2g fiber, 15.1g net carb), 3.9g protein, 171 calories.

Chocolate Cupcakes

These cupcakes are so delicious you can't tell they are made without any wheat or gluten. Top the cupcakes with chocolate or vanilla whipped cream frosting.

Chocolate Whipping Cream Frosting

½ cup (120 ml) heavy whipping cream
¼ teaspoon vanilla extract
1½ tablespoons (20 g) granulated sugar
1 tablespoon (6 g) unsweetened cocoa powder

Combine all of the frosting ingredients into a bowl. Whip until stiff peaks form. Place in the refrigerator until ready to put on the cupcakes. To make vanilla frosting simply leave out the cocoa powder.

Cake

2 (1 ounce/28 g) squares semi-sweet baking chocolate
2 tablespoons (28 g) butter, melted
½ cup (100 g) sugar
¼ teaspoon salt
½ teaspoon vanilla extract
1 tablespoon (15 ml) milk or coconut milk
3 eggs
¼ cup (32 g) coconut flour, sifted
¼ teaspoon baking powder

Preheat oven to 400°F (200°C or gas mark 6). Combine baking chocolate and butter in a saucepan over medium-low heat. Stirring frequently,

112

Chocolate Cupcakes with chocolate and vanilla frostings.

cook until the chocolate squares are completely melted. Remove from heat. Blend in sugar, salt, vanilla extract, milk, and eggs. Whisk in coconut flour and baking powder until batter is smooth. Pour batter into greased muffin cups (baking cups optional). Bake for 23 to 24 minutes. Remove from oven and let cool. Top with chocolate or vanilla whipped cream frosting.

Yield: 6 cupcakes
Per serving: 7.8g fat, 24.3g total carbohydrate (2.2g fiber, 22.1g net carb), 4g protein, 179 calories.

Chocolate Peanut Butter Cupcakes
If you like chocolate mixed with peanut butter, your will love these cupcakes. Peanut butter is used in both the cake batter and frosting to give these cupcakes a delightful peanut butter taste.

Frosting
1 (1 ounce/28 g) square semi-sweet baking chocolate
½ tablespoon (7 g) butter

½ cup (60 g) powdered sugar
⅓ cup plus 2 tablespoons (117 g) peanut butter
¼ teaspoon vanilla extract
2 teaspoons milk

Combine baking chocolate and butter in a saucepan over medium-low heat. Stirring occasionally, cook until the chocolate square is completely melted. Blend in remaining ingredients and set aside.

Cake
2 (1 ounce/28 g) squares semi-sweet baking chocolate
2 tablespoons (28 g) butter
3 tablespoons (49 g) chunky peanut butter
1 tablespoon (15 ml) milk or coconut milk
½ cup (100 g) sugar
¼ teaspoon salt
½ teaspoon vanilla extract
3 eggs
¼ cup (32 g) coconut flour, sifted
¼ teaspoon baking powder

Preheat oven to 400° F (200°C or gas mark 6). Combine baking chocolate and butter in a saucepan over medium-low heat. Stirring occasionally, cook until the chocolate squares are completely melted. Remove from heat. Blend in peanut butter, milk, sugar, salt, vanilla extract, and eggs. Whisk in coconut flour and baking powder until batter is smooth. Pour batter into greased muffin cups. Bake for 18 to 20 minutes. Remove from oven and let cool. Top with frosting.

Yield: 6 cupcakes
Per serving: 23.1g fat, 38.3g total carbohydrate (3.9g fiber, 34.4g net carb), 10.9g protein, 389 calories.

Chocolate Peppermint Cupcakes
The chocolate peppermint frosting makes these cupcakes irresistibly delicious.

Frosting
1 (1 ounce/28 g) square semi-sweet baking chocolate
½ tablespoon (7 g) butter
½ cup (60 g) powdered sugar
¾ teaspoon peppermint extract
¼ teaspoon vanilla extract
1 tablespoon (15 ml) milk

Combine baking chocolate and butter in a saucepan over medium-low heat. Stirring occasionally, cook until the chocolate square is completely melted. Blend in remaining ingredients and set aside.

Cake
2 (1 ounce/28 g) squares semi-sweet baking chocolate
2 tablespoons (28 g) butter
½ cup (100 g) sugar
¼ teaspoon salt
½ teaspoon vanilla extract
1 tablespoon (15 ml) milk or coconut milk
3 eggs
¼ cup (32 g) coconut flour, sifted
¼ teaspoon baking powder

Preheat oven to 400°F (200°C or gas mark 6). Combine baking chocolate and butter in a saucepan over medium-low heat. Stirring frequently, cook until the chocolate squares are completely melted. Remove from heat. Blend in sugar, salt, vanilla extract, milk, and eggs. Whisk in coconut flour and baking powder until batter is smooth. Pour batter into greased muffin cups. Bake for 23 to 24 minutes. Remove from oven and let cool. Top with frosting.

Yield: 6 cupcakes
Per serving: 10.6g fat, 18.9g total carbohydrate (2.2g fiber, 16.7g net carb), 4.5g protein, 187 calories.

Chocolate Strawberry Cupcakes

Who doesn't like strawberries and chocolate? This recipe combines them.

2 (1 ounce/28 g) squares semi-sweet baking chocolate
2 tablespoons (28 g) butter
½ cup (100 g) sugar
¼ teaspoon salt
½ teaspoon vanilla extract
1 tablespoon (15 ml) milk or coconut milk
3 eggs
¼ cup (32 g) coconut flour, sifted
¼ teaspoon baking powder
6 medium strawberries, chopped

Preheat oven at 400°F (200°C, or gas mark 6). Combine baking chocolate and butter in a saucepan over medium-low heat. Stirring frequently, cook until the chocolate squares are completely melted. Remove from heat. Blend in sugar, salt, vanilla extract, milk, and eggs. Whisk in coconut flour and baking powder until batter is smooth. Fold in strawberries. Pour batter into greased muffin cups. Bake for 23 to 25 minutes. Remove from oven and let cool. Eat as is or top with whipped cream or frosting of your choice.

Yield: 6 cupcakes
Per serving: 8.2g fat, 22.7g total carbohydrate (2g fiber, 20.7g net carb), 4g protein, 178 calories.

Chocolate Banana Nut Cupcakes

These cupcakes mix chocolate with banana and nuts—a winning combination!

Frosting

1 (1 ounce/28 g) square semi-sweet baking chocolate
½ tablespoons (7 g) butter
½ cup (60 g) powdered sugar

¼ teaspoon vanilla extract
1 tablespoon (15 ml) milk

Combine baking chocolate and butter in a saucepan over medium-low heat. Stirring occasionally, cook until the chocolate square is completely melted. Blend in remaining ingredients and set aside.

Cake

2 (1 ounce/28 g) squares semi-sweet baking chocolate
2 tablespoons (28 g) butter
½ cup (100 g) sugar
¼ teaspoon salt
½ teaspoon vanilla extract
1 tablespoon (15 ml) milk or coconut milk
3 eggs
¼ cup (32 g) coconut flour, sifted
¼ teaspoon baking powder
½ cup (75 g) peanuts, halves and wholes
½ medium banana, sliced and quartered

Preheat oven to 400°F (200°C or gas mark 6). Combine baking chocolate and butter in a saucepan over medium-low heat. Stirring frequently, cook until the chocolate squares are completely melted. Remove from heat. Blend in sugar, salt, vanilla extract, milk, and eggs. Whisk in coconut flour and baking powder until batter is smooth. Fold in peanuts and banana slices. Pour batter into greased muffin cups. Bake for 23 to 25 minutes. Remove from oven and let cool. Top with frosting.

Yield: 6 cupcakes
Per serving: 16.8g fat, 39.9g total carbohydrate (3.5g fiber, 36.4g net carb), 7.8g protein, 331 calories.

Candy Bar Cupcakes

These cupcakes taste very similar to Snickers candy bars.

3 eggs
1 tablespoon (15 ml) coconut oil or butter, melted

5 tablespoons (65 g) Sucanat or brown sugar
¼ cup (64 g) natural chunky peanut butter
¼ teaspoon salt
¼ teaspoon vanilla extract
¼ cup (32 g) sifted coconut flour
¼ teaspoon baking powder
½ cup (88 g) sweet milk chocolate chips

Preheat oven to 400°F (200°C or gas mark 6). Blend together eggs, oil, sugar, peanut butter, salt, and vanilla extract. Combine coconut flour with baking powder and whisk into batter until there are no lumps. Fold in chocolate chips. Pour into greased muffin cups. Bake for 15 minutes.

Yield: 6 cupcakes.
Per serving: 12.8g fat, 26.8g total carbohydrate (3.3g fiber, 23.5g net carb), 6.9g protein, 244 calories.

Rocky Road Cupcakes
The inspiration for this recipe comes from rocky road ice cream—chocolate ice cream with nuts and marshmallows. This recipe uses chocolate cake with nuts, but instead of marshmallows we use dried fruit. The recipe calls for either dried cherries or cranberries but almost any dried fruit will work.

2 (1 ounce/28 g) squares semi-sweet baking chocolate
2 tablespoons (28 g) butter
½ cup (100 g) sugar
¼ teaspoon salt
½ teaspoon vanilla extract
1 tablespoon (15 ml) milk or coconut milk
3 eggs
¼ cup (32 g) coconut flour, sifted
¼ teaspoon baking powder
¼ cup (28 g) chopped walnuts, pecans, or peanuts
¼ cup (30 g) dried cherries or cranberries
2 tablespoons (14 g) chopped walnuts, pecans, or peanuts, for topping

Preheat oven to 400°F (200°C or gas mark 6). Combine baking chocolate and butter in a saucepan over medium-low heat. Stirring frequently, cook until the chocolate squares are completely melted. Remove from heat. Blend in sugar, salt, vanilla extract, milk, and eggs. Whisk in coconut flour and baking powder until batter is smooth. Stir in ¼ cup (28 g) chopped nuts and fruit. Pour batter into greased muffin cups. Sprinkle 2 tablespoons (14 g) of chopped nuts on the top of each cupcake. Bake for 20 to 22 minutes.

Yield: 6 cupcakes
Per serving: 12.3g fat, 24.8g total carbohydrate (2.5g fiber, 22.3g net carb), 5.7g protein, 227 calories.

Bread and Butter Pudding

This dessert is a traditional favorite using day-old bread. It works exceptionally well with Leslie's Sandwich Bread (page 19). It is both a pudding and a cake or simply a pudding cake.

4 cups (440 g) Leslie's Sandwich Bread, torn into bite size pieces
½ teaspoon cinnamon
¼ teaspoon nutmeg
3 tablespoons (42 g) butter, melted
½ cup (75 g) raisins
3 eggs, lightly beaten
⅓ cup (69 g) sugar
2¼ cups (530 ml) milk
Cinnamon and sugar for topping

Put bread pieces into a 1½ quart (1½ liter) casserole dish. Sprinkle cinnamon, nutmeg, and butter over the bread and mix. Add raisins. Beat eggs, sugar, and milk together. Pour egg mixture over the bread. Let stand at room temperature for 1 hour.

Preheat oven to 350°F (180°C or gas mark 4). Set casserole in a large, shallow pan and pour in hot water to a depth of 1 inch (2.5 cm). Bake uncovered for about 1 hour and 10 minutes or until a knife inserted in the center comes out clean. Sprinkle the top with a little granulated sugar and cinnamon. Cool slightly and serve.

Yield: 12 servings
Per serving: 6.2g fat, 19.3g total carbohydrate (1g fiber, 18.3g net carb), 4.1g protein, 150 calories.

Variation: For a more fruity combination add to the batter ½ cup (75 g) chopped apple and ½ cup (60 g) chopped walnuts.

Apricot Almond Bread Pudding

Apricots and almonds always go well together. In this recipe they make the perfect complement. Fully ripened apricots impart an intense flavor and sweetness but even slightly unripe, tart apricots will develop a rich flavor when baked.

8 ounces (225 g) day-old Leslie's Sandwich Bread (page 19)
1 teaspoon cinnamon
¼ cup (56 g) butter, melted
3 eggs, beaten
½ cup (100 g) sugar
¼ cup (85 g) honey
1 teaspoon vanilla extract
½ teaspoon almond extract
1½ cups (295 ml) milk
1 pound (455 g) apricots, pitted and halved if small or quartered if large
½ cup (55 g) sliced almonds

Use day-old bread that is beginning to dry out. If the bread is not dry, toast it lightly. Break it into ½ inch (6 mm) pieces and put it into a 1½ quart (1½ liter) baking dish. Sprinkle cinnamon and melted butter over the bread and mix. Beat eggs, sugar, honey, vanilla extract, almond extract, and milk together. Pour egg mixture over the bread. Let stand at room temperature for 1 hour.

Preheat oven to 350°F (180°C or gas mark 4). Stir apricots into mixture. Sprinkle top with almonds. Set baking dish into a large, shallow pan and pour in hot water to a depth of 1 inch (2.5 cm). Bake uncovered for about 1 hour and 10 minutes or until a knife inserted in the center comes out clean. Cool slightly and serve topped with whipped cream.

Yield: 12 servings
Per serving: 8.5g fat, 24.4g total carbohydrate (1.8g fiber, 22.6g net carb), 4.4g protein, 183 calories.

Apple Tart

Tarts are baked dishes consisting of a pastry base with a filling and an open top which is not covered by pastry. The pastry is often a thin pie-like crust, but can be thicker like cake. This tart and the others in this chapter use a cake base. The filling is more like a topping on the cake.

Apple Topping

2 tart apples, peeled, cored, and thinly sliced
2 teaspoons lemon juice
1 teaspoon cinnamon
¼ teaspoon nutmeg
¼ cup (25 g) sugar
1 teaspoon cornstarch

Mix all the topping ingredients together in a small saucepan and cook over medium heat. Stir frequently until mixture thickens. Remove from heat and set aside.

Cake

3 eggs
2 tablespoons (30 ml) whole milk or coconut milk
¼ cup (25 g) sugar
¼ teaspoon salt
¼ teaspoon almond extract
¼ cup (55 g) butter, melted
¼ cup (32 g) coconut flour, sifted
2 tablespoons (20 g) brown rice flour
½ teaspoon baking powder

Preheat oven to at 375°F (190°C or gas mark 5). In a mixing bowl, whisk together eggs, milk, sugar, salt, almond extract, and butter. Whisk in coconut flour. Combine brown rice flour and baking powder and stir into wet mixture. Pour batter evenly into a greased 8 inch (20 cm) or 9 inch (23 cm) pie dish. Spread topping over batter. Bake for 30 minutes.

Yield: 8 servings
Per serving: 8g fat, 17.7g total carbohydrate (2.8g fiber, 14.4g net carb), 3.1g protein, 151 calories.

Cherry Tart

Cherry Topping
1 can (14.5 ounces/430 g) pitted tart cherries
⅓ cup (33 g) sugar
4 teaspoons cornstarch
⅛ teaspoon almond extract

Drain the liquid from the cherries into a small saucepan and set aside the cherries. Stir sugar and cornstarch into the cherry juice and cook over medium heat. Stir continually until mixture thickens.

Remove from heat. Stir in almond extract and cherries.

Prepare the cake according to the Apple Tart directions (page 121) and replace the apple topping with the cherry topping. Cook as directed in the Apple Tart recipe. Remove from oven and let cool. Top with whipped cream before serving.

Yield: 8 servings
Per serving: 8g fat, 28.8g total carbohydrate (1.9g fiber, 26.9g net carb), 3.2g protein, 196 calories.

Pear Tart

This recipe was inspired by Gail Simmons, the host of television's *Top Chef: Just Desserts*. She says that when she was growing up one of her favorite treats was the pear tart her mother made. This pear tart is similar to her mother's recipe but has a few changes, including replacing the wheat flour with coconut flour. It is delicious. I can see why it was a favorite.

Pear Topping
2 pears, cored and sliced ½ inch (12 mm) thick
2 teaspoons lemon juice
1 teaspoon cinnamon
¼ teaspoon nutmeg
¼ cup (25 g) sugar
1 tablespoon (8 g) cornstarch

Mix all the topping ingredients together in a small saucepan and cook over medium heat. Stir frequently until mixture thickens. Remove from heat and set aside.

Prepare the cake according to the Apple Tart directions (page 121) and replace the apple topping with the pear topping. Cook as directed in the Apple Tart recipe.

Yield: 8 servings
Per serving: 8g fat, 19.5g total carbohydrate (3.3g fiber, 16.2g net carb), 3.2g protein, 158 calories.

Strawberry Tart

Strawberry Topping
2 cups (340 g) sliced strawberries
2 teaspoons lime juice
¼ cup (25 g) sugar
1 tablespoon (8 g) cornstarch

Mix all the topping ingredients together in a small saucepan and cook over medium heat. Stir frequently just until mixture begins to thicken, but do not overcook. Remove from heat and set aside.

Prepare the cake according to the Apple Tart directions (page 121) and replace the apple topping with the strawberry topping. Cook as directed in the Apple Tart recipe.

Yield: 8 servings
Per serving: 8.1g fat, 15g total carbohydrate (2.4g fiber, 12.6g net carb), 3.3g protein, 143 calories.

Peach Tart

Peach Topping
2 cups (340 g) sliced peaches (canned or fresh)
2 teaspoons lemon juice
¼ cup (25 g) sugar
½ teaspoon cinnamon
1 tablespoon (8 g) cornstarch

Mix all the topping ingredients together in a small saucepan and cook over medium heat. If you are using canned peaches, drain the fruit first. Stir frequently just until mixture begins to thicken, but do not overcook. Remove from heat and set aside.

Prepare the cake according to the Apple Tart directions (page 121) and replace the apple topping with the peach topping. Cook as directed in the Apple Tart recipe.

Yield: 8 servings
Per serving: 8g fat, 15.8g total carbohydrate (2.2g fiber, 13.6g net carb), 3.4g protein, 146 calories.

Mixed Berry Tart

Berries make an excellent topping for tarts. This recipe calls for a mix of berries (raspberries, blackberries, and blueberries) but you can also use the same recipe using any one of these berries.

Mixed Berry Topping

2 cups (290 g) mixed berries (raspberries, blackberries, blueberries)
2 teaspoons lime juice
¼ cup (50 g) sugar
1 tablespoon (8 g) cornstarch

Mix all the topping ingredients together in a small saucepan and cook over medium heat. Stir frequently just until mixture begins to thicken, but do not overcook. Remove from heat and set aside.

Prepare the cake according to Apple Tart directions (page 121) and replace the apple topping with the mixed berry topping. Cook as directed in the Apple Tart recipe. Remove from oven and let cool. Top with whipped cream before serving.

Yield: 8 servings
Per serving: 8.2g fat, 19.2g total carbohydrate (3.9g fiber, 15.3g net carb), 3.5g protein, 160 calories.

Cinnamon Pecan Tart

These tarts have a taste similar to coffee cake. They're one of my favorites. Serve with a scoop of vanilla ice cream for a taste sensation.

Cinnamon Pecan Topping

¾ cup (82 g) pecans, chopped
¼ cup (40 g) coconut sugar or brown sugar
½ teaspoon cinnamon
¼ cup (55 g) butter, melted

Mix all the topping ingredients together in a bowl and set aside.

Prepare the cake according to the Apple Tart directions (page 121) and replace the apple topping with the cinnamon pecan topping. Cook as directed in the Apple Tart recipe.

Yield: 8 servings
Per serving: 20.9g fat, 13.9g total carbohydrate (2.5g fiber, 11.4g net carb), 4g protein, 252 calories.

6

Cookies and Snacks

Cookies make simple, tasty desserts and snacks. We include several traditional favorites such a Sugar Cookies and Snickerdoodles as well as variations on familiar cookies such as Raisin Cookies, Chocolate Pecan Sandies, and Almond Butter Cookies. We've also included a number of unique and original recipes such as Cardamom Cookies, Coconut Pecan Yum Yums, Orange Delights, M&M Almond Cookies, and Gufan Fruit Bars. You will also find fruit- and cream-filled sandwich cookies, including Chocolate Sandwich Cookies that are filled with whipped cream or ice cream and frozen to produce delicious little ice cream sandwiches.

Also included are non-cookie snacks which are both sweet and savory such as Cinnamon Crisps, Coconut Banana Bites, Sausage Balls, and Hush Puppies Supreme.

Sugar Cookies

These cookies are rolled in sugar crystals. For a festive appearance use red or blue colored sugar crystals. If you don't have sugar crystals, you can substitute with granulated sugar. It's not as colorful, but tastes just as good.

4 eggs
¾ cup plus 2 tablespoons (76 g) sugar
½ teaspoon vanilla extract
¼ teaspoon salt
½ cup (112 g) butter, melted
¾ cup (96 g) coconut flour, sifted
Sugar crystals

Preheat oven to 375°F (190°C or gas mark 5). Combine eggs, sugar, vanilla extract, salt, and butter and mix well. Stir in coconut flour. Let batter rest for 5 minutes to allow it to thicken. Form dough into walnut size balls and roll in sugar crystals, coating thoroughly. Place on cookie sheet 1-inch apart, then flatten each ball to a diameter of about 2 inches. Bake for 15 minutes.

Yield: 2 dozen cookies
Per cookie: 5.1g fat, 5.5g total carbohydrate (1.4g fiber, 4.1g net carb), 1.5g protein, 73 calories.

Sugar Cookies.

Snickerdoodles

Topping
1 tablespoon plus 2 teaspoons (12 g) cinnamon
¼ cup (50 g) granulated sugar for topping

Combine cinnamon with ¼ cup of granulated sugar, and set aside.

Dough
4 eggs
¾ cup plus 2 tablespoons (76 g) sugar
½ teaspoon vanilla extract
¼ teaspoon salt
½ cup (112 g) butter, melted
¾ cup (96 g) coconut flour, sifted

Preheat oven to 375°F (190°C or gas mark 5). Combine eggs, sugar, vanilla extract, salt, and butter and mix well. Stir in coconut flour. Let batter rest for 5 minutes to allow it to thicken. Form dough into walnut size balls and roll in cinnamon topping, coating thoroughly. Place on cookie sheet 1-inch apart, then flatten each ball to a diameter of about 2 inches. Bake for 14 to 15 minutes.

Yield: 2 dozen cookies
Per cookie: 5.1g fat, 8g total carbohydrate (1.7g fiber, 6.3g net carb), 1.5g protein, 82 calories.

Cardamom Cookies

Cardamom is a spice frequently used in India. It is found in both sweet and savory dishes. These cookies have a mildly exotic flavor.

4 eggs
1 cup (200 g) sugar
½ teaspoon vanilla extract
¼ teaspoon salt
½ cup (112 g) butter, melted
¾ cup (96 g) coconut flour, sifted
½ cup (100 g) granulated sugar for coating
1 tablespoon plus 1 teaspoon (8 g) cardamom
1 teaspoon cinnamon

Preheat oven to 375°F (190°C or gas mark 5). Combine eggs, 1 cup (200 g) sugar, vanilla extract, salt, and butter and mix well. Stir in coconut flour. Let batter rest for 5 minutes to allow it to thicken. In a separate bowl, combine ½ cup (100 g) granulated sugar with cardamom and cinnamon. This will be used for the coating. Form dough into walnut size balls and roll in the coating thoroughly. Place on cookie sheet 1-inch apart, then flatten each ball to a diameter of about 2 inches. Bake for 15 minutes.

Yield: 2 dozen cookies.
Per cookie: 5.1g fat, 15.2g total carbohydrate (1.6g fiber, 13.6g net carb), 1.5g protein, 110 calories.

Peppermint Cookies

These make great treats for the Christmas holidays. Crushed hard peppermint candies or candy canes are added to the batter make this a really sweet treat.

4 eggs
1 cup (200 g) sugar
½ teaspoon peppermint extract
½ teaspoon vanilla extract
¼ teaspoon salt
½ cup (112 g) butter, melted
¾ cup (96 g) coconut flour, sifted
3 tablespoons (20 g) crushed peppermint candy
Granulated sugar for coating

Preheat oven to 375°F (190°C or gas mark 5). Combine eggs, sugar, peppermint extract, vanilla extract, salt, and butter and mix well. Stir in coconut flour. Crush peppermint candy into rice size pieces and stir into batter. Let batter rest for 5 minutes to allow it to thicken. Form dough into walnut size balls and roll in granulated sugar. Place on cookie sheet 1-inch apart, then flatten each ball to a diameter of about 2 inches. Bake for 15 minutes.

Yield: 2 dozen cookies.
Per serving: 5.1g fat, 11.5g total carbohydrate (1.4g fiber, 10.1g net carb), 1.5g protein, 97 calories.

Almond Cookies

4 eggs
1 cup (200 g) sugar
1 teaspoon almond extract
¼ teaspoon salt
½ cup (112 g) butter, melted
½ cup (56 g) almond meal
¾ cup (96 g) coconut flour, sifted
Sugar for coating
¼ cup (28 g) sliced or slivered almonds

Preheat oven to 375°F (190°C or gas mark 5). Combine the first five ingredients and mix well. Stir in almond meal, then the coconut flour. Let batter rest for 5 minutes to allow it to thicken. Form dough into walnut size balls and roll in sugar. Place on cookie sheet 1-inch apart, then flatten each ball to a diameter of about 2 inches. Top each cookie with sliced or slivered almonds. Bake for 15 minutes.

Yield: 2 dozen cookies
Per cookie: 6.8g fat, 11.4g total carbohydrate (1.8g fiber, 9.6g net carb), 2.3g protein, 113 calories.

Almond M&M Cookies

These cookies are made with M&M's candies. The recipe calls for plain M&M's, but if you prefer a nuttier cookie you can use peanut or almond M&M's. If you use the latter, increase M&M's to ½ cup (100 g).

4 eggs
1 cup (200 g) sugar
1 teaspoon almond extract
¼ teaspoon salt
½ cup (112 g) butter, melted
½ cup (56 g) almond meal
¾ cup (96 g) coconut flour, sifted
¼ cup (50 g) plain M&M's candies
Almond meal for coating

Preheat oven to 375°F (190°C or gas mark 5). Combine the first five ingredients and mix well. Stir in almond flour followed by coconut flour. Fold in the M&Ms. Let the batter rest for 5 minutes to allow it to thicken. Form dough into walnut size balls and roll in almond meal, coating thoroughly. Place on cookie sheet 1-inch apart, then flatten each ball to a diameter of about 2 inches. Bake for 15 minutes.

Yield: 2 dozen cookies
Per cookie: 6.4g fat, 11.8g total carbohydrate (1.7g fiber, 10.1g net carb), 2g protein, 111 calories.

Coconut Pecan Yum Yums

These cookies contain pecans, coconut, and milk chocolate chips—yum, yum!

4 eggs
1 cup (150 g) loosely packed brown sugar or coconut sugar
2 tablespoons (26 g) granulated sugar
½ teaspoon vanilla extract
¼ teaspoon salt
1 cup (220 g) butter, melted
¾ cup (96 g) coconut flour, sifted
½ teaspoon baking powder
½ cup (55 g) chopped pecans
½ cup (45 g) flaked coconut
¼ cup (44 g) sweet milk chocolate chips

Preheat oven to 350°F (180°C or gas mark 4). Whisk together eggs, sugars, vanilla extract, salt, and butter until blended. Combine coconut flour with baking powder and whisk into wet ingredients. Stir in pecans,

133

coconut, and chocolate chips. Let the batter rest for a few minutes to allow it to thicken. Drop the batter by the spoonful onto a greased cookie sheet at least 1 inch (2.5 cm) apart. Bake for 17 to 18 minutes.

Yield: about 30 cookies
Per cookie: 9g fat, 9.2g total carbohydrate (1.5g fiber, 7.7g net carb), 1.6g protein, 121 calories.

Chocolate Sandwich Cookies

These cookies are filled with whipped cream and put in the freezer. Once the whipped cream freezes, they can be eaten like miniature ice cream sandwiches. If you like, you can substitute softened vanilla ice cream for the whipped cream. Freeze before serving.

Filling

1 cup (240 ml) heavy cream
1 teaspoon vanilla extract
¼ cup (52 g) granulated sugar

Whip cream until soft peaks form. Add vanilla extract and gradually add in sugar and whip until stiff peaks form. Put into the refrigerator until ready to use.

Cookie Dough

1¼ cups (220 g) semisweet chocolate chips
½ cup (110 g) butter
6 eggs
1 cup (200 g) sugar
1 teaspoon vanilla extract
½ teaspoon salt
1 cup (128 g) coconut flour, sifted

Preheat oven to 350°F (180°C or gas mark 4). Combine chocolate chips with butter in a saucepan and cook over medium-low heat, stirring frequently, until chocolate is completely melted. Blend the chocolate and butter together until evenly mixed. Set aside to cool.

Whisk together eggs, sugar, vanilla extract, and salt until blended. Whisk in chocolate mixture. Combine coconut flour with baking powder and whisk into batter. Let the batter rest for a few minutes to allow it to thicken. Drop the batter by the spoonful

onto a greased cookie sheet about 2 inches (5 cm) apart. (Note: Use two baking sheets and place all the batter on the two baking sheets at the same time, but cook the cookies one sheet at a time. If you use only one baking sheet and wait for the first batch of cookies to cook, the unused batter in the bowl will thicken even more. If this happens, roll the batter into balls and flatten them on the baking sheet.) Bake for 12 minutes.

Remove from oven and let cool briefly. While still hot, remove the cookies from the baking sheet and place them on a cooling rack. When cool, put whipping cream on the bottom of one cookie and sandwich it between another cookie. Do this to all the cookies. Place the cookies in the freezer for at least 2 hours or until the whipped cream has frozen.

Yield: about 16 sandwich cookies
Per cookie: 13.1g fat, 28.9g total carbohydrate (3.3g fiber, 25.6g net carb), 4.4g protein, 249 calories.

Variation: Add ½ cup of semisweet chocolate chips to the batter before baking. Cook as directed.

Chocolate Pecan Sandies

½ cup (88 g) semisweet chocolate chips
¼ cup (55 g) butter
3 eggs
½ cup (100 g) sugar
¼ teaspoon almond extract
¼ teaspoon salt
½ cup (64 g) coconut flour, sifted
½ cup (55 g) chopped pecans

Preheat oven to 350°F (180°C or gas mark 4). Combine chocolate chips and butter in a saucepan and cook over medium-low heat, stirring frequently, until chocolate is completely melted. Blend the chocolate and butter together until evenly mixed. Set aside to cool. Whisk together eggs, sugar, almond extract, and salt until blended. Whisk in chocolate mixture. Combine coconut flour with baking powder and whisk into batter. Stir in pecans. Let the batter rest for a few minutes to allow it to thicken. Drop the batter by the spoonful onto a greased cookie sheet about 2 inches (5 cm) apart. Bake for 12 minutes.

Yield: about 16 cookies
Per cookie: 8.3g fat, 12.3g total carbohydrate (1.9g fiber, 10.4g net carb), 2.4g protein, 131 calories.

Almond Butter Cookies

4 eggs
1 cup (200 g) sugar
½ cup (110 g) butter, melted
½ teaspoon almond extract
¼ teaspoon salt
½ cup (64 g) raw almond butter
½ teaspoon baking powder
¾ cup (96 g) coconut flour, sifted

Preheat oven to 350°F (180°C or gas mark 4). Whisk together eggs, sugar, butter, almond extract, and salt until blended. Whisk in almond butter. Combine coconut flour with baking powder and stir into batter. Let the batter rest for a few minutes to allow it to thicken. Drop the batter by the spoonful onto a greased cookie sheet about 2 inches (5 cm) apart. Bake for 16 to 17 minutes.

Yield: about 2 dozen cookies
Per cookie: 6.6g fat, 11.2g total carbohydrate (1.5g fiber, 9.7g net carb), 1.9g protein, 109 calories.

136

Raisin Cookies

4 eggs
1 cup (200 g) sugar
½ cup (110 g) butter, melted
1 teaspoon vanilla extract
¼ teaspoon salt
½ cup (64 g) raw almond butter
½ teaspoon baking powder
¾ cup (96 g) coconut flour, sifted
1 cup (145 g) raisins
1 teaspoon cinnamon
½ teaspoon allspice

Preheat oven to 350°F (180°C or gas mark 4). Whisk together eggs, sugar, butter, vanilla extract, and salt until blended. Whisk in almond butter. Combine coconut flour with baking powder and stir into batter. Stir in raisins, cinnamon, and allspice. Let the batter rest for a few minutes to allow it to thicken. Drop the batter by the spoonful onto a greased cookie sheet about 2 inches (5 cm) apart. Bake for 16 to 17 minutes.

Yield: about 2 dozen cookies
Per serving: 6.6g fat, 16.1g total carbohydrate (1.8g fiber, 14.3g net carb), 2.1g protein, 128 calories.

Fruit and Cream Sandwich Cookies
These cookie sandwiches are filled with whipped cream and jam. The recipe specifies strawberry or blackberry jam, but any flavor of jam will work.

Filling
1 cup (240 ml) heavy cream
1 teaspoon vanilla extract
2 tablespoons (26 g) sugar
1 cup (160 g) strawberry or blackberry jam

Whip cream until soft peaks form. Add vanilla extract, then gradually add sugar and jam and whip until stiff peaks form. Set aside.

Cookie Dough

4 eggs
1 cup (200 g) sugar
½ cup (110 g) butter, melted
1 teaspoon vanilla extract
¼ teaspoon salt
½ cup (64 g) raw almond butter
½ teaspoon baking powder
¾ cup (96 g) coconut flour, sifted

Preheat oven to 350°F (180°C or gas mark 4). Whisk together eggs, sugar, butter, vanilla extract, and salt until blended. Whisk in almond butter. Combine coconut flour with baking powder and stir into batter. Let the batter rest for a few minutes to allow it to thicken. Drop the batter by the spoonful onto a greased cookie sheet about 2 inches (5 cm) apart. Bake for 16 to 17 minutes.

Remove the cookies from the baking sheet and let cool completely. Spread the filling on the bottom side of one cookie and sandwich the filling with a second cookie. Repeat with all the cookies. Put the cookies in the freezer for at least 2 hours or until the filling is frozen. Serve cold. For variety, replace the cream filling with flavored ice cream such as strawberry, coconut, or pralines and cream.

Yield: 14 cookies
Per cookie: 12.1g fat, 28.6g total carbohydrate (2.6g fiber, 26g net carb), 3.4g protein, 233 calories.

Gufan Fruit Bars

Gufan is an acronym for "Ground-Up Fruit and Nuts." These fruit bars require no baking and are very simple to make.

1 cup (120 g) dried cranberries
½ cup (65 g) dried apricots
1 cup (170 g) pitted dates
1 cup (120 g) chopped walnuts

½ cup (142 g) orange juice concentrate, no water added
¼ cup (32 g) coconut flour

Using a food processor, grind the first four ingredients together. Put the fruit and nut mixture into a mixing bowl and stir in orange juice concentrate and coconut flour until blended. Press into a greased 8 x 8 x 2-inch (20 x 20 x 5-cm) pan. Chill overnight. Cut into bars and serve.

Yield: 20 (2 x 2 ½-inch/5 x 6-cm) bars
Per cookie: 3.8g fat, 9.7g total carbohydrate (2g fiber, 7.7g net carb), 2g protein, 751 calories.

Cranberry Walnut Cookies

4 eggs
1 cup (200 g) sugar
½ cup (110 g) butter, melted
1 teaspoon vanilla extract
1 tablespoon plus 1 teaspoon (24 g) orange juice concentrate, no water added
¼ teaspoon salt
½ cup (64 g) raw almond butter
½ teaspoon baking powder
¾ cup (96 g) coconut flour, sifted
1 cup (120 g) dried cranberries
1 cup (120 g) chopped walnuts

Preheat oven to 350°F (180°C or gas mark 4). Whisk together eggs, sugar, butter, vanilla extract, orange juice concentrate, and salt until blended. Whisk in almond butter. Combine coconut flour with baking powder and stir into batter. Stir in cranberries and walnuts. Let the batter rest for a few minutes to allow it to thicken. Drop the batter by the spoonful onto a greased cookie sheet about 2 inches (5 cm) apart. Bake for 16 to 18 minutes.

Yield: about 30 cookies
Per cookie: 7.6g fat, 9.9g total carbohydrate (1.7g fiber, 8.2g net carb), 2.5g protein, 114 calories.

Orange Delights

The orange buttercream frosting is what makes these cookies stand out.

Orange Buttercream Frosting

½ cup (112 g) butter, softened
½ teaspoon vanilla extract
1 tablespoon (18 g) orange juice concentrate, no water added
1 tablespoon (7 g) very finely chopped orange peel
1¼ cups (150 g) powdered sugar
Dash of salt

Using an electric mixer, cream the butter. Add the remaining ingredients and blend together until smooth.

Cookie Dough

4 eggs
1 cup (200 g) sugar
½ cup (110 g) butter, melted
½ teaspoon vanilla extract
¼ teaspoon salt
½ cup (64 g) raw almond butter
½ teaspoon baking powder
¾ cup (96 g) coconut flour, sifted

Preheat oven to 350°F (180°C or gas mark 4). Whisk together eggs, sugar, butter, vanilla extract, salt, and almond butter until blended. Combine coconut flour with baking powder and stir into batter. Let the batter rest for a few minutes to allow it to thicken. Drop the batter by the spoonful onto a greased cookie sheet about 2 inches (5 cm) apart. Bake for 16 to 17 minutes.

Remove the cookies from the oven and put them on a cooling rack. Once they are cool, top with frosting.

Yield: about 2 dozen cookies
Per cookie: 10.4g fat, 17.6g total carbohydrate (1.5g fiber, 16.1g net carb), 2g protein, 168 calories.

Almond Enjoy Bars

If you like Almond Joy or Bounty candy bars, you will love these tasty treats. Sweetened coconut wrapped in a coating of chocolate is hard to beat.

¼ cup (32 g) coconut flour
3 tablespoons (42 g) coconut oil
½ cup plus 2 tablespoons (148 ml) coconut milk
⅛ teaspoon almond extract
¼ cup (85 g) honey
1½ cups (125 g) shredded or flaked coconut
½ cup (60 g) chopped almonds, lightly roasted
1 cup (175 g) semi-sweet chocolate chips
2 tablespoons (26 g) sugar
¼ cup plus 3 tablespoons (105 ml) heavy cream

In a medium size bowl, mix together coconut flour and coconut oil. Stir in coconut milk, honey, and almond extract. As you add the coconut milk, the flour will expand as it soaks up the liquids and the volume will increase significantly. Stir in shredded coconut and almonds. Form the batter into 16 little bars about 2 inches (5 cm) long and ¾ inch (2 cm) tall and place them on a dish or cutting board covered with wax paper. Put the bars, dish and all, into the freezer for at

least 1 hour. This will harden the bars, making them easier to coat with chocolate.

In a medium saucepan, heat cream, chocolate chips, and sugar, stirring constantly, until the chocolate melts. Do not boil. Remove from heat and blend the ingredients until you have a thick, evenly textured chocolate syrup. Let cool to room temperature.

Remove the coconut bars from the freezer. Pick up a bar, and coat the bar evenly with chocolate on all sides using a table knife. Place the bar back onto the wax paper. Repeat with each bar until they are all coated. Let the bars sit in the refrigerator overnight to allow the chocolate coating to dry. The longer they sit, the dryer the chocolate will become and the less messy the bars will be to eat.

Yield: 16 bars
Per serving: 11.4g fat, 16.3g total carbohydrate (2.5g fiber, 13.8g net carb), 2.5g protein, 171 calories.

Cinnamon Crisps

These cookie-like snacks are made with day-old bread. If you have fresh bread on hand, slice it and dry it out before using. Use Leslie's Sandwich Bread or the Artisan Sandwich Bread described in Chapter 2. These snacks actually taste better as they age, so after baking, let them sit for 4 to 12 hours before eating. This allows the flavors to thoroughly blend and the bread to crisp up.

6 slices of Leslie's Sandwich Bread (page 19), sliced
½ cup (112 g) butter, melted
¼ cup (50 g) sugar
1 tablespoon (7 g) ground cinnamon

Preheat the oven to 325°F (170°C or gas mark 3). Cut the sliced bread into 1½ to 2 inch (3 to 5 cm) squares. Put the melted butter in a small bowl. Mix the sugar and cinnamon together, then pour the mixture onto a dinner plate or pie dish. Dip both sides of each slice of bread into the butter. Make sure each side is thoroughly coated with butter. Dip the bread into the cinnamon sugar mixture, coating both sides. Place the coated bread on a cookie sheet. Bake for 25 minutes. Remove from the oven and place on a cooling rack. The bread will become crisper as they cool. Let the bread sit for at least 4 hours before eating, they taste better with age. Store leftovers in an airtight container.

Yield: about 30 cookies
Per cookie: 3.9g fat, 6.4g total carbohydrate (0.6g fiber, 5.8g net carb), 0.7g protein, 62 calories.

Coconut Banana Bites

These little crunchy snacks cook up quick and taste delicious. Great for parties or as an after-school treat.

1 egg
½ cup (120 ml) water
¼ teaspoon salt
3 tablespoons (60 g) honey
½ cup plus 1 tablespoon (75 g) CGF flour (page 16)
1 cup (85 g) flaked or shredded coconut
2 medium bananas, cut into 1 inch (2.5 cm) slices
Coconut oil for frying

Whisk together egg, water, salt, honey, and CGF flour until there are no lumps. Stir in coconut flakes. Preheat coconut oil in a deep fryer to 350°F (180°C). Dip banana slices into the batter and spoon one slice at a time into hot coconut oil. Cook until the batter turns a golden brown. Remove from the hot oil and cool on a paper towel.

Yield: about 18 banana bites
Per banana bite: 2.1g fat, 9.6g total carbohydrate (1.2g fiber, 8.4g net carb), 0.9g protein, 58 calories.

Hush Puppies Supreme

Hush puppies are deep fried seasoned corn batter. They make a nice appetizer, side dish, or snack. This recipe contains no corn meal but does have corn kernels. These are the best hush puppies we have ever eaten, thus the designation "Supreme."

2 eggs
1 cup (240 ml) ice cold water
¾ cup (136 g) CGF Flour Mix (page 16)
½ cup plus 2 tablespoons (75 g) millet flour
1 teaspoon baking powder
½ teaspoon salt
1 teaspoon onion powder
½ cup (80 g) finely chopped onion

½ cup (68 g) whole kernel corn
3 tablespoons (27 g) finely chopped jalapeno pepper
Coconut oil for frying

Whisk together egg and cold water. Combine CGF Flour Mix, millet flour, baking powder, salt, and onion powder and stir into egg mixture. Stir in onion, corn, and jalapeno pepper. Drop batter by the spoonful into hot coconut oil and deep fry until golden brown, about 4 minutes. Drain on a paper towel.

Yield: about 20 hush puppies
Per hush puppy: 2.2g fat, 7.3g total carbohydrate (0.5g fiber, 6.8g net carb), 1.5g protein, 53 calories.

Sausage Balls
Sausage balls are a traditional southern dish in the USA. This version uses coconut flour in place of wheat flour. Sausage balls make good hors d'oeuvres, appetizers, or snacks and can even be served as part of a main meal accompanied by a side dish of vegetables.

2 eggs
¼ teaspoon salt
⅛ teaspoon black pepper
3 tablespoons (24 g) coconut flour, sifted
¼ teaspoon baking powder
½ pound (225 g) ground sausage (pork or turkey)
4 ounces (115 g) sharp cheddar cheese, shredded

Preheat oven to 400°F (200°C or gas mark 6). Whisk together eggs, salt, and pepper. Combine coconut flour and baking powder and whisk into egg mixture. Using your hands, mix the sausage and shredded cheese a little at a time into the batter until thoroughly mixed. Form the dough into small walnut size balls and place on a greased cooking sheet. Bake in preheated oven for 15 minutes.

Yield: 15 sausage balls
Per sausage ball: 7.6g fat, 1.1g total carbohydrate (0.6g fiber, 0.5g net carb), 5.8g protein, 97 calories.

Meats and Main Dishes

Our favorite use of coconut flour is for making savory dishes and main courses. These often but not always include meat, fish, or poultry. Most of the recipes in this chapter can be served as a main course, though a few can make great side dishes or accompaniments. For example, the Turkey Stuffing recipe generally accompanies a roast turkey as a side dish, but with the addition of a little chopped turkey and gravy, it becomes a main course. Recipes in this chapter use either coconut flour or the CGF Flour Mix. The CGF Flour Mix makes an excellent coating for fried meats and vegetables. It also makes an excellent crust for calzones.

Pan-Fried Chicken

This recipe makes great gluten-free crispy fried chicken. Adjust the seasoning as desired to suit your own tastes.

1 egg, beaten
⅓ cup (43 g) coconut flour, sifted
⅓ cup (43 g) cornstarch
1 teaspoon salt
1 teaspoon black pepper
1 teaspoon paprika
1 teaspoon onion powder
1 teaspoon chili powder
Coconut oil for frying
8 small chicken breasts or 8 thighs (70 g each)

In a bowl, mix together coconut flour, cornstarch, salt pepper, paprika, onion powder, and chili powder. Fill a deep skillet with ¼ inch (6 mm) of oil and heat over medium heat. Dip each piece of chicken into the beaten egg, then roll it into the flour mixture, coating both sides. Carefully place each piece into the hot skillet. Cook covered for 8 to 15 minutes or until well browned; cooking time will vary depending on the size of the chicken. Turn and cook uncovered until the other side is browned and juices run clear. Remove from skillet and drain on paper towel before serving.

Yield: 8 servings
Per serving: 6.6g fat, 8.4g total carbohydrate (2.1g fiber, 6.3g net carb), 21.8g protein, 186 calories.

Sesame Pecan Chicken with Hoisin Sauce

Hoisin Dipping Sauce
¼ cup (60 ml) soy sauce
2 tablespoons (32 g) natural peanut butter
1 tablespoon (20 g) honey
2 teaspoons rice vinegar or coconut vinegar
1 garlic clove, finely minced
⅛ teaspoon black pepper
1 teaspoon Chinese hot sauce (optional)

Combine all ingredients in a small mixing bowl. Whisk until well blended.

Chicken
2 eggs
1 cup (110 g) Leslie's Bread Crumbs (page 26)
½ cup (55 g) finely chopped pecans
¼ cup (24 g) sesame seeds
1 teaspoon paprika
1 teaspoon salt
1 cup (240 ml) coconut oil
1 pound (455 g) boneless chicken breasts cut into 1-inch wide strips

Beat eggs until frothy. In a separate bowl, combine bread crumbs, pecans, sesame seeds, paprika, and salt. Heat coconut oil in a large skillet over medium high heat. Dip the chicken strips in the eggs and then roll the strips in the bread crumb mixture, pressing to help it adhere to the meat. Cook the chicken until dark golden brown, about 4 or 5 minutes per side. Serve with hoisin dipping sauce.

Yield: 6 servings
Per serving: 22.2g fat, 40.5g total carbohydrate (11.8g fiber, 28.7g net carb), 35.1g protein, 500 calories.

Tempura Shrimp and Vegetables

Here is an excellent tempura recipe you can use for deep-fried shrimp as well as vegetables. This recipe makes outstanding onion rings, but can also be used with zucchini, carrots, mushrooms, and other vegetables.

1 egg
2 teaspoons soy sauce
½ cup (120 ml) ice-cold water
½ cup (64 g) CGF Flour Mix (page 16)
2 tablespoons (16 g) tapioca flour
¼ teaspoon baking powder
¼ teaspoon salt
½ teaspoon onion powder
18 large shrimp, peeled and deveined with tails on
Coconut oil for frying

Whisk together egg, soy sauce, and cold water. Combine CGF baking mix, tapioca flour, baking powder, salt, and onion powder and stir into egg mixture. Batter should be thick enough to cling to the shrimp. Dip shelled shrimp or vegetables into the batter and deep fry at about 350°F (180°C) until golden brown. Fry only a few at a time to keep the foods from sticking together while cooking. Drain on a paper towel, add a little salt if desired, and enjoy.

Yield: 18 shrimp
Each: 2.3g fat, 6.3g total carbohydrate (0.4g fiber, 5.9g net carb), 1.8g protein, 52 calories.

Coconut Shrimp

This is a variation of the Tempura Shrimp recipe. Follow the directions for the Tempura Shrimp recipe above and add ½ cup (40 g) shredded or desiccated coconut to the batter. Cook as directed.

Yield: 18 shrimp
Each: 3g fat, 6.6g total carbohydrate (06g fiber, 6g net carb), 1.8g protein, 60 calories.

Cashew Chicken

This is similar to the cashew chicken served at Chinese restaurants with some notable differences. More vegetables are used and the chicken is battered and deep fried.

1 egg, beaten
¼ cup plus 2 tablespoons (88 ml) cup ice-cold water
½ cup (68 g) CGF Flour Mix (page 16)
½ teaspoon baking powder
1 teaspoon salt, divided in half
8 ounces (227 g) chicken breast, cut into bite size pieces
Coconut oil for frying
1 cup (160 g) chopped onion
1 cup (150 g) chopped bell pepper
2 cups (142 g) chopped broccoli
1 tablespoon (8 g) cornstarch or tapioca flour
1 cup (235 ml) chicken stock or water
4 medium mushrooms, sliced
8 ounces (140 g) bamboo shoots, drained
½ tablespoon (20 g) honey
2 tablespoons (30 ml) soy sauce
2 tablespoons (30 ml) rice or coconut vinegar (optional)
⅔ cup (63 g) cashews, toasted

Preheat oven to 250°F (120°C or gas mark ½). The oven is used to keep the cooked chicken warm until the dish is ready to serve.

Mix together beaten egg, water, CGF Flour Mix, baking powder, and ½ teaspoon salt. Dip chicken into batter and deep fry at about 350°F (180°C) in coconut oil until golden brown. Drain on a paper towel and place in a warm oven while you complete the

recipe. You may also refry the chicken for a minute or so just before serving to heat it up and make it crispier.

Heat some coconut oil in a skillet and sauté onions, bell pepper, and broccoli until the onions start to turn translucent. Mix the corn starch with the chicken stock and stir into the skillet. Add mushrooms and bamboo shoots and continue to cook until mushrooms are soft and mixture thickens. Add honey, soy sauce, rice vinegar, and ½ teaspoon salt and remove from heat. Stir in cashews, top with cooked chicken and serve.

Yield: 8 one cup (188 g) servings
Per serving: 3.2g fat, 8g total carbohydrate (2.3g fiber, 5.7g net carb), 2.7g protein, 128 calories.

Stuffed Bell Peppers

4 bell peppers
2 tablespoons (28 g) butter
1 pound (455 g) ground beef, pork, or turkey
1 cup (160 g) chopped onion
1 cup (100 g) chopped celery
2 cloves garlic, diced
1 cup (70 g) chopped mushrooms
1 teaspoon salt
½ teaspoon cayenne pepper
2 cups (230 g) Leslie's Bread Crumbs (page 26)
½ cup (58 g) shredded cheddar cheese

Preheat oven to 375°F (190°C or gas mark 5). Cut green or red bell peppers in half lengthwise. Scoop out and discard the seeds and veins. Set aside.

In a skillet, melt butter and cook meat, onions, celery, and garlic on medium heat until the vegetables are crisp tender. Add mushrooms, salt and cayenne pepper and cook another 1 to 2 minutes. Remove from heat and stir in bread crumbs, allowing the bread to absorb all the juices in the skillet. Spoon the mixture into the cavity of each bell pepper half, filling them as full as possible. Sprinkle cheese on top. Place the peppers in a baking dish and bake for 40 minutes.

Yield: 8 stuffed peppers
Each: 10.5g fat, 32.7g total carbohydrate (5.3g fiber, 27.4g net carb), 22.8g protein, 322 calories.

Cajun Chicken Fingers

This chicken tastes better than KFC! It is also better for you since it does not contain trans fats or MSG and is cooked in healthy coconut oil. This recipe calls for 3 tablespoons of Cajun seasoning (a mixture of paprika, garlic powder, onion powder, black pepper, cayenne pepper, oregano, and thyme). Some brands of seasoning mix are spicier than others, so you can adjust the Cajun seasoning to your preferences or make your own using an equal part of each ingredient listed above.

2 large (300 g) boneless chicken breasts
1 egg
½ cup plus 2 tablespoons (150 ml) ice-cold water

153

½ cup (64 g) CGF Flour Mix (page 16)
3 tablespoons (29 g) Cajun seasoning mix
½ teaspoon salt
1 teaspoon onion powder
½ teaspoon baking powder
Coconut oil for frying

Cut chicken breasts into 3 to 4 inch (8 to 10 cm) long strips. Set aside.
Whisk together egg and cold water. Combine CGF Flour Mix, Cajun seasoning, salt, onion powder and baking powder and stir into egg mixture. Dip chicken pieces into the batter and deep fry at about 350°F (180°C) in coconut oil until golden brown, about 4 minutes. Drain on a paper towel, add a little salt if desired, and enjoy.

Yield: about 15 chicken fingers
Each: 3.9g fat, 3.7g total carbohydrate (0.4g fiber, 3.3g net carb), 6.7g protein, 78 calories.

Sweet and Sour Pork

This recipe can be made using either boneless pork or chicken. It tastes great either way. The sweet taste comes from a mixture of sugar and fruit. The sour comes from vinegar. The recipe calls for rice or coconut vinegar, however, for a fruitier flavor you can substitute a fruit-flavored vinegar such as raspberry, orange, or pomegranate vinegar.

1 pound (455 g) boneless pork or chicken
1 egg
1 teaspoon soy sauce
½ cup (120 ml) ice-cold water
½ cup plus 2 tablespoons (86 g) CGF Flour Mix (page 16)
½ teaspoon salt
½ teaspoon baking powder
Coconut oil for frying
1 red or green bell pepper, chopped
1 cup (160 g) chopped onion
1 medium carrot, sliced
6 medium to large mushrooms, sliced

1½ cups (360 ml) chicken broth or water
½ cup (8 ounces/85 g) pineapple chunks
2 tablespoons (30 ml) soy sauce
3 tablespoons (45 ml) rice or coconut vinegar
3 tablespoons (26 g) sugar
2 tablespoons (16 g) cornstarch or tapioca flour

Preheat oven to 250°F (120°C or gas mark ½). The oven is used to keep the cooked meat warm until the dish is ready to serve.

Cut pork or chicken into 1 inch (2.5-cm) cubes and set aside. Whisk together egg, soy sauce, and cold water. Combine CGF Flour Mix, salt, and baking powder and stir into egg mixture. Dip meat pieces into the batter and deep fry at about 350°F (180°C) in coconut oil until golden brown, about 3 minutes. Drain on a paper towel and set aside.

In a large skillet, sauté bell pepper, onion, and carrot pieces until the onions start to become translucent. Add mushrooms, then stir in 1 cup (240 ml) of chicken broth, pineapple, soy sauce, vinegar, and sugar. Bring to a boil, then reduce heat to keep the mixture at a simmer. Blend cornstarch in ½ cup (120 ml) of chicken broth or water and stir into skillet. Cook and stir until thickened. Remove from heat.

Deep fry the meat pieces a second time for about 1 minute. This will warm them up and make them crispier. Combine fried meat and sauce and serve with hot cooked rice.

Yield: 8 one cup (216 g) servings
Per serving: 6.8g fat, 19g total carbohydrate (2.2g fiber, 16.8g net carb), 18.5g protein, 216 calories.

Zucchini Boats

2 large zucchini
2 tablespoons (30 g) coconut oil
½ pound (225 g) ground beef
1 cup (160 g) chopped onion
4 garlic cloves, diced
1 teaspoon salt
¼ teaspoon black pepper

1 cup (110 g) Leslie's Bread Crumbs (page 26)
1 egg, beaten
½ cup (130 g) salsa
1 cup (115 g) shredded Monterey Jack or cheddar cheese

Preheat oven to 375°F (190°C or gas mark 5). Cut zucchini in half lengthwise. Using a spoon, start about ½ inch (1.25 cm) from the end of the zucchini and scoop out the flesh from the center of the zucchini, leaving the hollowed-out shells. The walls on the shells should be about ¼ inch (0.75 cm) thick. Reserve the hollowed-out flesh.

In a skillet, add coconut oil and cook meat, onions, garlic, and zucchini flesh and

cook until meat is lightly browned and the onions are crisp tender. Remove from heat. Stir in salt, black pepper, and bread crumbs. Mix, allowing the bread to absorb all the juices in the skillet. Stir in beaten egg, salsa, and ½ cup (55 g) of cheese. Spoon the mixture into the cavity of each zucchini half, filling them as full as possible. Sprinkle the remaining cheese on top. Place the zucchini boats in a baking dish and bake for 40 minutes before serving.

Yield: 4 zucchini boats
Each: 22.6g fat, 36.3g total carbohydrate (5.7g fiber, 30.6g net carb), 30.3g protein, 467 calories.

Zucchini Fritters

1 small zucchini, shredded
1 tablespoon (10 g) chopped red onion
3 tablespoons (23 g) shredded Monterey Jack cheese
⅛ teaspoon cayenne pepper
1 teaspoon dried tarragon
½ teaspoon onion powder
¼ teaspoon salt
2 eggs
2 tablespoons (16 g) coconut flour, sifted
Coconut oil for frying
Sour cream

In a bowl, combine zucchini, onion, cheese, cayenne, tarragon, onion powder, and salt. Set aside. In another bowl, whisk eggs until blended. Whisk in coconut flour until batter is smooth. Stir in zucchini mixture. Fill a skillet with about ⅛ inch (3 mm) of coconut oil and heat over medium heat. Spoon batter onto the hot skillet and immediately flatten and spread the batter evenly to a diameter of about 3 to 4 inches (7.5 to 10 cm). Cook until the underside is a deep golden brown, turn, and cook the other side. Repeat with the remaining batter, adding more oil as needed. Serve topped with a spoonful of sour cream.

Yield: 6 fritters
Each: 4.7g fat, 2.5g total carbohydrate (1.2g fiber, 1.3g net carb), 3.4g protein, 65 calories.

Eggs Foo Yum

This recipe is patterned after the traditional Eggs Foo Young served in Chinese restaurants. This version incorporates coconut flour and chicken to give it more body and flavor.

3 eggs
2 tablespoons (16 g) coconut flour, sifted
½ cup (70 g) diced cooked chicken

½ cup (35 g) finely chopped bok choy or napa cabbage
2 tablespoons (10 g) finely chopped onion
3 medium mushrooms, finely chopped
¼ cup (70 g) drained and chopped bamboo shoots
2 tablespoons (80 g) finely chopped red bell pepper
2 teaspoons soy sauce
¼ teaspoon salt
¼ teaspoon ground ginger
Coconut oil for frying

In a bowl, whisk eggs until blended. Whisk in coconut flour until batter is smooth. Stir in remaining ingredients. Fill a skillet with about ⅛ inch (3 mm) of coconut oil and heat over medium heat. Spoon batter onto the hot skillet and immediately flatten and spread the batter evenly to a diameter of about 3½ to 4 inches (8 to 10 cm). Cook until the underside is a deep golden brown, then turn and cook the other side. Repeat with the remaining batter, adding more oil as needed.

Yield: 6 servings
Per serving: 4.5g fat, 3.8g total carbohydrate (1.7g fiber, 2.1g net carb), 7.5g protein, 85 calories.

Mighty-Good Meatloaf

1 pound (455 g) ground beef
2 eggs
1 cup (160 g) finely chopped onion
¾ cup (195 g) salsa
1 teaspoon salt
¼ teaspoon black pepper
2 cups (240 g) shredded cheddar cheese, divided in half
1 cup (115 g) Leslie's Bread Crumbs (page 26)
¼ cup (60 g) tomato sauce
2 tablespoons (40 g) honey

Preheat oven to 350°F (180°C or gas mark 4). In a large bowl, combine meat, eggs, onion, salsa, salt, and black pepper. Using your hands, thoroughly mix these ingredients together. Mix in 1 cup (120 g) of cheese and bread crumbs until just blended. Form the mixture into a loaf and place in a lightly greased baking dish. Mix together the tomato sauce and honey and pour over the top of the meatloaf. Sprinkle the remaining 1 cup (120g) of cheese over the top of the sauce. Bake for 1 hour.

Yield: about 10 (4 oz/115 g) servings
Per serving: 12.1g fat, 8.9g total carbohydrate (1g fiber, 7.9g net carb), 21.8g protein, 219 calories.

Pig in a Blanket

If you like to eat hot dogs but can't handle gluten, here is the answer for you. Most gluten-free hot dog buns are oversized and tasteless. These hot dogs are wrapped and cooked in a tasty gluten-free roll. You get just the right amount of bread for your hot dog.

1 tablespoon fast-acting yeast
2 tablespoons (26 g) sugar
1 cup plus 2 tablespoons (270 ml) very warm water
2½ cups (340 g) CGF Flour Mix (page 16)

1 teaspoon baking powder
1 tablespoon (9 g) xanthan gum
1 teaspoon salt
3 eggs
2 tablespoon (28 g) coconut oil, melted
12 hot dogs

Make the dough using the first 9 ingredients above according to the directions for Preparing the Dough on page 17.

Rub your hands with a little coconut oil to prevent sticking and form the dough into 12 equal size balls. Roll each ball in a little CGF flour mix to coat the outside. Place the dough balls on a greased baking sheet and flatten them into a rectangular shape large enough to wrap around a hot dog. Place a hot dog along one edge of each dough blanket and roll them up. Dip your fingers in flour to prevent sticking as you wrap the blanket around the hot dogs. Seal the two edges of the dough blanket. If the two sides don't stick together you can pin them in place by inserting a toothpick.

Put the wrapped hot dogs in a warm place and allow the dough to double in thickness. Preheat the oven to 350°F (180°C or gas mark 4). Bake for about 15 to 16 minutes or until the bread covering is lightly browned. Serve with mustard, pickle relish, and other traditional hot dog condiments.

Yield: 12 servings
Per serving: 21.6g fat, 27g total carbohydrate (3.4g fiber, 23.6g net carb), 9.9g protein, 341 calories.

Variation: Pour a scoop of chili with beans and shredded cheddar cheese over the pig in a blanket for a great-tasting chili dog.

Corned Beef Delight
This is a delicious corned beef main dish cooked on the stovetop. Use thinly sliced deli corned beef or ham.

3 eggs
¼ teaspoon salt

1 teaspoon Dijon mustard
2 tablespoons (16 g) coconut flour, sifted
3 to 4 ounces (85 to 115 g) thinly sliced corned beef or ham
2 cups (60 g) fresh spinach
3 ounces (85 g) Gouda, Colby, or Swiss cheese, shredded
½ teaspoon dill

Stir together eggs, salt, and mustard in a bowl. Add coconut flour and whisk together until batter is smooth, then set aside. Put enough oil in a skillet to coat the bottom and place over medium heat. Layer corned beef over the entire bottom of the pan. Layer the spinach evenly over the beef. Pour batter over the spinach, spreading it out evenly. Cover the batter with shredded cheese. Sprinkle dill over the top. Cover and cook for about 10 minutes or until the batter is cooked and puffy. Serve hot.

Yield: 4 servings
Per serving: 15.2g fat, 3.7g total carbohydrate (1.9g fiber, 1.8g net carb), 14.5g protein, 210 calories.

Turkey Stuffing

For those who are going gluten free, a good turkey stuffing is one of the foods that is sorely missed. Here is a delicious gluten-free version that is sure to please. It's also a good way to make use of day-old bread.

4 cups (440 g) Leslie's Sandwich Bread (page 19) cut in cubes
½ cup (112 g) butter
½ pound (225 g) ground sausage
1 cup (160 g) chopped onion
1 cup (100 g) chopped celery
4 medium mushrooms, chopped
½ teaspoon salt
¼ teaspoon black pepper
1 teaspoon sage
1 teaspoon crushed rosemary

Preheat oven to 300°F (150°C or gas mark 2). Cube enough of Leslie's Sandwich Bread to make about 4 cups (440 g) of bread cubes. Place on

161

a baking sheet and bake for about 20 minutes or until the bread is dry and a light golden brown. Remove from oven. The bread cubes can be made several hours or even a day beforehand if desired.

Melt butter in a large skillet over medium heat. Add sausage, onion, and celery. Cook until meat is browned. Add mushrooms, salt, black pepper, sage, and rosemary and cook until vegetables are tender. Stir in dried bread cubes, allowing them to soak up all the juices and butter. Once the juices are absorbed, remove from heat and let cool. Fill turkey or chicken cavity with stuffing. Roast the stuffed bird as per directions. Put the remaining stuffing in a small casserole dish and set aside until the bird is almost finished cooking. Put the uncovered casserole dish in the oven with the turkey for about 15 minutes to heat. Combine with the stuffing in the bird and serve together.

Yield: about 12 half cup (100 g) servings
Per serving: 14.3g fat, 9.2g total carbohydrate (1g fiber, 8.2g net carb), 5.2g protein, 184 calories.

Gluten-Free Calzones

Calzones are pizzas that are folded in half and baked. Traditionally, calzones are filled with typical pizza toppings like mozzarella cheese, sausage, pepperoni, mushrooms, and the like. However, they can be stuffed with any type of filling. The directions below include the basic crust and several different fillings. One of our favorites is patterned after the popular Philadelphia cheesesteak sandwich. Another filling is scrambled eggs, sausage, and cheese, which makes a delicious breakfast.

Calzones can be frozen and reheated, so you can make several and keep some for later. To reheat, let the calzone defrost, then cook in a preheated oven at 350°F (180°C or gas mark 4) for about 12 to 15 minutes. Prepare ahead of time for a quick breakfast in the morning or for easy lunches and dinners. Calzones take a little longer to prepare than many of the other recipes in this book but they are well worth it.

Crust

1 tablespoon (8.5 g) fast-acting yeast
2 tablespoons (26 g) sugar

1 cup plus 2 tablespoons (265 ml) very warm water
2¼ cups (300 g) CGF Flour Mix (page 16)
1 tablespoon (9 g) xanthan gum
1½ teaspoons salt
2 teaspoons onion powder
3 eggs
2 tablespoons (28 g) butter, melted
2 cups (225 g) shredded cheddar or Monterey Jack cheese

This recipe makes enough for six calzones. Make the dough using the ingredients above following the directions for Preparing the Dough on page 17. Note that when making the dough, the 2 cups (225 g) of cheddar or Monterey Jack cheese is to be added with the other ingredients in the mixing bowl.

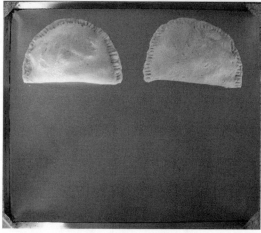

Once the dough is made, rub your hands with coconut oil to prevent sticking and form the dough into 6 equal size balls. Roll each ball in a little CCF Flour Mix to coat the outside. Place one dough ball in the upper left quarter of a greased baking sheet and a second ball in the right quarter. Using a rolling pin, flatten each ball to about 5½ inches (14 cm) wide and about 7 inches (18 cm) long. Put the recommended amount of filling into the upper half of each. Dip your fingers in water and wet the outside rim of the dough. Gently fold the lower half of the dough up and over the filling. Moistening the outside rim allows the dough to seal together when joined. For the remaining four balls of dough it is easier to roll them out, one at a time, on a sheet of wax paper and then transfer them to the baking sheet before filling. Carefully remove and discard the wax paper. Moisten the edges and fill the shells as described

above. Although it will be snug, all six calzones will fit on a standard size baking sheet.

Put the calzones in a warm place to allow the dough to rise until the shells double in thickness. Preheat the oven to 375°F (190°C or gas mark 5). Bake for about 15 minutes or until the crusts are a golden brown. Remove the calzones from the baking sheet and place them on a wire rack to cool. This will prevent the bottom of the calzones from sweating and becoming soggy.

Leftover cal-zones can be stored in the refrigerator for a day or so, or frozen for extend periods of time. To reheat leftover unfrozen calzones put them directly on the wire rack in a toaster oven at 350°F (180°C or gas mark 4) for 12 to 14 minutes. Defrost frozen calzones before reheating.

164

Pizza Filling

There are an endless variety of pizza combinations and everybody has their favorites. Use the following ingredient list as a guide to create your favorite combinations.

1 pound (455 g) sausage
1 cup (160 g) chopped onion
½ cup (75 g) chopped bell pepper
2 cloves garlic, finely chopped
6 medium mushrooms, chopped
2 tablespoons (9 g) oregano
2 tablespoons (9 g) basil
1 teaspoon salt
¼ cup (20 g) shredded parmesan cheese
¾ cup (180 g) tomato sauce
8 ounces (225 g) cheese (mozzarella, Munster, Colby, or Monterey Jack)
¾ cup (90 g) shredded cheddar cheese, for topping

In a skillet, cook sausage, onion, bell peppers, and garlic until the sausage browns and onions start to become translucent. Add mushrooms, oregano, basil, and salt and cook another minute or two. Remove the skillet from heat and let cool. Fill the calzone shells with the meat mixture. Sprinkle 2 teaspoons of parmesan cheese, 2 tablespoons (30 g) tomato sauce, and one-sixth (1.3 ounces/38 g) of the cheese on top of the filling in each calzone. Seal the calzones and let them rise. Sprinkle 2 tablespoons (16 g) of cheddar cheese on top, and cook as directed above.

Yield: 6 calzones
Per ½ calzone: 30.5g fat, 27.2g total carbohydrate (4.4g fiber, 22.8g net carb), 23.8g protein, 436 calories.

Philadelphia Cheesesteak Filling

1 pound (455 g) chopped or ground beef
½ cup (80 g) chopped onion
⅓ cup (50 g) chopped green pepper
4 medium mushrooms, chopped
1½ cups (170 g) shredded Monterey Jack cheese

2 tablespoons (18 g) chopped jalapeno peppers (optional)
Salt and black pepper to taste
¾ cup (90 g) shredded Monterey Jack cheese, for topping

In a skillet, cook beef, onions, and green pepper until the beef is browned and the vegetables are crisp tender. Add mushrooms and jalapeno peppers and continue cooking for another 3 or 4 minutes or until most of the juices have evaporated. Drain grease and excess juices and discard. Season with salt and black pepper to taste. Set aside to cool.

Put one-sixth of the filling into the upper half of each shell, fold over, seal, and let rise. Before cooking, sprinkle about 2 tablespoons (16 g) of shredded Monterey Jack cheese on the top of each calzone. Cook as directed.

Yield: 6 calzones
Per ½ calzone: 20g fat, 24.8g total carbohydrate (3.4g fiber, 21.4g net carb), 25.6g protein, 382 calories.

Chicken Broccoli Filling
¼ cup (56 g) butter
1 pound (455 g) chicken, cut into small bite size pieces
1 cup (160 g) chopped onion
2½ cups (115 g) finely chopped broccoli
1 teaspoon salt
½ teaspoon black pepper
¾ cup (170 g) cottage cheese
6 ounces (170 g) cheddar cheese, cut into cubes, for filling
¾ cup (90 g) shredded cheddar cheese, for topping

Heat butter in a skillet and cook chicken, onions, and broccoli until the chicken turns white and the onions start to turn translucent. Add salt and pepper, remove from heat, and let cool. Stir in cottage cheese and cheddar cheese. Fill the calzone shells with the meat mixture. Seal the calzones and let them rise. Before cooking, sprinkle 2 tablespoons (16 g) of shredded cheddar cheese on top of each calzone and cook as directed.

Yield: 6 calzones

166

Per ½ calzone: 23.1g fat, 26.1g total carbohydrate (4.3g fiber, 21.8g net carb), 28g protein, 423 calories.

Ham and Eggs Filling

9 eggs, beaten
9 ounces (258 g) ham, cut into ¼-inch (5-mm) cubes
Salt and black pepper to taste
6 ounces (190 g) Monterey Jack cheese, for filling
¾ cup (90 g) shredded Monterey Jack cheese, for topping

In a skillet, cook eggs and ham until the eggs are no longer runny. Add salt and pepper to taste. Let cool. Put one-sixth of the egg mixture and 1 ounce (30 g) of cheese in each shell, fold over, seal, and let rise. Before cooking, sprinkle about 2 tablespoons (16 g) of shredded Monterey Jack cheese on the top of each calzone. Cook as directed.

Yield: 6 calzones
Per ½ calzone: 23.3g fat, 24.8g total carbohydrate (3.4g fiber, 21.4g net carb), 21.9 protein, 394 calories.

Sausage and Eggs Filling

9 eggs, beaten
9 ounces (258 g) sausage
Salt and black pepper to taste
¾ cup (195 g) salsa
6 ounces (190 g) Monterey Jack cheese, for filling
¾ cup (90 g) shredded Monterey Jack cheese, for topping

In a skillet, cook eggs and sausage until the sausage is browned and the eggs are no longer runny. Remove from heat and add salsa and salt and pepper to taste. Let cool. Put one-sixth of the egg mixture and 1 ounce (30 g) of cheese in each shell, fold over, seal, and let rise. Before cooking, sprinkle about 2 tablespoons (16 g) of shredded Monterey Jack cheese on the top of each calzone. Cook as directed.

Yield: 6 calzones
Per ½ calzone: 27.1g fat, 24.9g total carbohydrate (3.4g fiber, 21.5g net carb), 22.7g protein, 432 calories.

Ham and Cheese Filling

15 ounces (450 g) ham, cut into ¼-inch (5-mm) cubes
9 ounces (260 g) cheddar cheese, for filling
¾ cup (90 g) shredded cheddar cheese, for topping

Put 2½ ounces (75 g) of ham and 1½ ounces (43 g) of cheese in each shell, fold over, seal, and let rise. Before cooking, sprinkle about 2 tablespoons (16 g) of shredded cheddar cheese on the top of each calzone. Cook as directed.

Yield: 6 calzones
Per ½ calzone: 23.3g fat, 25.2g total carbohydrate (3.4g fiber, 21.8g net carb), 21.9g protein, 397 calories.

Barbecue Beef or Chicken Filling

1 pound (455 g) of meat (steak, ground beef, chicken, pork), cut into bite size pieces
1 cup (160 g) chopped onion
½ cup (75 g) chopped bell pepper
½ teaspoon salt
¾ cup (190 g) barbecue sauce

In a skillet, cook meat, onion, and bell pepper until onions start to turn translucent. Remove from heat and stir in salt and barbecue sauce. Put one-sixth of the meat mixture in each shell, fold over and seal. Cook as directed.

Yield: 6 calzones
Per ½ calzone: 12.8g fat, 30.8g total carbohydrate (3.4g fiber, 27.4g net carb), 20.1g protein, 320 calories.

Chicken and Zucchini Casserole
(Savory Bread Pudding)

In the process of developing new recipes we often wonder if some of the foods that are normally sweet or eaten as desserts can be transformed into sugar-free or savory versions. This is how we developed many of

the savory pancakes, waffles, and muffins in this book. Bread pudding is traditionally eaten as a dessert, but it need not be sweet or confined to the dessert category. Here is a savory bread pudding that is tasty enough to serve as a main dish. Rather than calling it a pudding, we call it a casserole, which is a more accurate name.

8 ounces (225 g) day-old Leslie's Sandwich Bread (page 19)
1½ cups (295 ml) milk
1½ pounds (180 g) zucchini, shredded
2 tablespoons (28 g) extra virgin olive oil or coconut oil
12 ounces (340 g) chicken breast, cut into bite size pieces
1 small or ½ medium onion, chopped
2 garlic cloves, diced
¼ teaspoon celery seed
1 teaspoon dill
1 teaspoon basil
½ teaspoon salt
¼ teaspoon black pepper
4 eggs
1½ cups (180 g) shredded cheddar cheese

Use day-old bread that is beginning to dry out. If the bread is not dry, toast it lightly. Break it into ½ inch (6 mm) pieces and put it into a 1½ quart (1½ liter) baking dish. Mix in milk and set aside for 1 hour, stirring occasionally. While the bread is soaking, place the shredded zucchini in a colander and salt generously. Toss and let sit in a colander in the sink for 15 minutes, then squeeze out any remaining water. Add olive oil to a large skillet and cook the chicken, onion, and garlic for about 2 minutes or until the onions start to become translucent. Stir in the zucchini and continue cooking for another 5 minutes or until the squash becomes limp. Stir in celery seed, dill, basil, salt, and black pepper. Remove from heat and add to the soaking bread.

Preheat oven to 350°F (180°C or gas mark 4). Beat the eggs and then stir them into the zucchini bread mixture. Stir in ½ cup (58 g) of shredded cheese. Sprinkle the remaining cheese over the top. Bake for 1 hour and 10 minutes.

Yield: 14 half cup (110 g) servings
Per serving: 9.3g fat, 5.4g total carbohydrate (0.4g fiber, 5g net carb), 13.8g protein, 160 calories.

Salmon Patties

3 eggs at room temperature
3 tablespoons (24 g) coconut flour, sifted
¼ teaspoon salt
⅛ teaspoon black pepper
¼ teaspoon dill
¼ cup (30 g) diced celery
¼ cup (40 g) diced onion
1 teaspoon grated lemon peel
6 ounces (170 g) cooked salmon
Coconut oil for frying

In a mixing bowl, whisk together eggs, and coconut flour. Stir in salt pepper, dill, celery, onion, lemon peel, and salmon. Use a generous amount of coconut oil for frying. Spoon batter into hot skillet and flatten to about ½ inch (1.25 cm) thick. Cook until bottom is a deep golden brown, then flip and cook the other side. Serve with tartar or cocktail sauce.

Yield: 6 patties
Each: 6.6g fat, 4.5g total carbohydrate (2.4g fiber, 2.1g net carb), 10g protein, 120 calories.

New England Clam Chowder with Dumplings

A classic dish originating in San Francisco is clam chowder served in a hollowed-out loaf of sourdough bread. If you make the Artisan Sandwich Bread (page 22) you can create a similar dish that is gluten-free (divide the dough into 4 individual loaves before baking). In this version, however, we miniaturized the bread into little dumplings that can be added on top of the chowder like you would add oyster crackers.

Dumplings

2 teaspoons fast-acting yeast
1 tablespoon (13 g) sugar
½ cup plus 2 tablespoons (150 ml) very warm water
1½ cups (200 g) CGF Flour Mix (page 16)
¼ teaspoon baking powder
2 teaspoons xanthan gum
1 teaspoon salt
2 eggs
¼ cup (56 g) butter, melted

To make the dough for the dumplings use the ingredients above and follow the directions for Preparing the Dough on page 17.

Rub your hands with a little coconut oil to prevent sticking and divide and form the dough into about 40 equal size balls. Place the balls onto a baking sheet and let rise until they double in size.

171

Preheat the oven to 350°F (180°C or gas mark 4). Bake for 15 minutes or until the dumplings are golden brown.

Yield: 40 dumplings
Each: 1.5g fat, 2.6g total carbohydrate (0.4g fiber, 2.4g net carb), 0.7g protein, 25 calories.

Chowder

3 tablespoons (42 g) butter
1 cup (160 g) finely chopped onion
1 cup (120 g) finely chopped celery
2 medium russet potatoes, chopped
1 jar (8 oz/235 ml) clam juice
½ teaspoon salt
½ teaspoon black pepper
1 can (10 oz/280 g) whole baby clams
2 tablespoons (16 g) cornstarch or tapioca flour
½ cup (120 ml) water
1½ cup (360 ml) heavy cream
4 teaspoons fish sauce (optional)

Using a 2 quart (2 liter) saucepan, heat the butter and sauté the onion and celery until the onion starts to become translucent. Add the potatoes, clam juice, salt, pepper, and the liquid from the can of clams and simmer for 30 minutes. Mix the corn starch in water and stir into the hot mixture. Cook, stirring, until the mixture begins to thicken. Pour in cream and fish sauce and continue to cook until the chowder thickens, stirring frequently. Do not boil. Remove from heat. Serve in bowls topped with dumplings.

Yield: 12 half cup (125 g) servings
Per serving: 4.5g fat, 11.8g total carbohydrate (1.3g fiber, 10.5g net carb), 3.1g protein, 98 calories.

Index